R<u>ock & Stro</u>ll

A Walk Around London's Greatest Hits

Jon Askew

w·w

Worthy-Words

Rock & Stroll - A Walk Around London's Greatest Hits
by Jon Askew

Worthy-Words 1-7-358-22

Copyright © Jon Askew 2022

Jon Askew asserts his right under the
Copyright, Designs and Patents Act of 1988
to be identified as the author of this work

All rights reserved
No reproduction without permission

Cover design consultant: Erin Askew-Hunt

First edition published March 2022
This edition published November 2022

ISBN: 979-8408203734

Product ref: 906261/05

To Erin

Thank you for listening

Jon Askew was born in Bedford, England, in 1964, and has written articles and poetry for numerous magazines. While not writing, he divides his time between playing guitar to capacity crowds around the world's greatest concert arenas, and coming to terms with his moderate musical talent and delusional fantasies of rock stardom. Rock & Stroll is his first book.

Contents

Intro - London Rocks..............................1

1 - Spiritual Sunrise..............................7

2 - Zebragate..28

3 - Anthem for Doomed Yoof..............37

4 - Juke Box Fury.................................46

5 - Merchant of Menace.......................58

6 - It's a Hard Rock Life.......................75

7 - Mourning Glory...............................97

8 - Caffeine Hit...................................110

9 - Squaring the Circle.......................124

10 - Rock of Ages...............................140

11 - What a North and South!.............152

12 - Pigs Might Fly.............................170

13 - Eclectic Avenue...........................184

14 - London's Brilliant Parade............200

15 - Waterloo Sunset..........................216

Outro - London Pride.........................237

Acknowledgements............................239

Bibliography.......................................241

Bonus Track.......................................242

Rock & Stroll

Intro
London Rocks

London. London Town. The City of London. LDN. Greater London. The Big Smoke. Cockneyville. The Capital City of the United Kingdom. Call it whatever you will - it's certainly been called a lot worse, especially by residents of the UK's other major cities.

But even they would have to acknowledge, albeit grudgingly, London's importance to the world of rock music. And as this little cluster of nations has led the way in popular music for decades, punching well above its weight to become a musical global superpower, some might even be bold enough to declare London as the world capital of rock and pop.

Admittedly, that is a very brave declaration as there are other major world cities, particularly in America, that could also stake a claim to that title, as well as here in the UK - most notably Liverpool and Manchester - and their claims are certainly all valid. But even several of the biggest bands and performers from those locations based themselves in London and would readily admit to having found inspiration for much of their music in the city.

Rock & Stroll

London's influence on the songs and images of pop culture has endured throughout many years and was especially strong during what was undoubtedly the golden age of British rock and pop music: the 1960s, '70s and '80s. They truly were the years that Britannia ruled the airwaves. These were particularly turbulent times however, both socially and politically, as during the 1960s the UK had not yet fully recovered from the terrible consequences of World War II and was struggling to regain its confidence and direction after years of gloomy post-war austerity. The effects of this were still causing desolation and dejection in large parts of the country, much of which continued through the 1970s and into the 1980s with industrial disputes, disrupted manufacturing, economic recession and civil unrest.

But despite this widespread discontent, there was also a growing sense in the sixties of exciting times ahead as the UK gradually rebuilt, redefined and then re-established itself, providing an increasing optimism that proved to be a rich source of material for musicians and songwriters to get their teeth into.

This optimistic outlook was especially strong among the baby boomer generation whose aspirations to a more upbeat future, coupled with a growing confidence in their own freedom of expression, led to a constant craving for new music they could claim for themselves. Britain was also becoming more open and multicultural, bringing increased awareness and exposure to music with different sounds and diverse themes. This in turn enhanced music's ability to effect the social, personal and political change that shapes much of what we know so well today.

Rock & Stroll

Add to this the huge developments in technology that became available for the creation and production of original material and all these elements came together to generate an urgent and voracious appetite for new music. This was a time when a three minute song on the radio had the power to change the world, and that power resulted in the emergence of many different genres that seemed to spawn with almost every weekly chart rundown. And London found itself at the very heart of this surge in pop culture.

So why is London so influential? What has inspired generations of singers and songwriters from all the different music genres to immortalise it? From Noel Coward's 'London Pride' and Ralph McTell's 'Streets of London', to artists as diverse as Bucks Fizz, The Pogues, Roy Hudd, Ranking Dread and The Wombles.

London is an enigma - a city of contradictions. It's homely yet heartless; vibrant yet violent; prosperous yet poverty stricken; delightful but deviant; sociable yet solitary. It manages to be historic while also being futuristic, seamlessly mixing wild new trends with traditions that haven't changed in centuries. It's a melting pot of diverse cultural influences that readily accepts new ideas in art and music despite its reputation for cold aloofness. It has some beautiful sights, but these are often set against a backdrop of grimy deprivation. It's gritty, and it can be ugly.

But it's these very contradictions that provide songwriters and musicians with a never ending stream of new ideas to write about. Music has an inherent power to inspire and excite, to comfort and console, to divide or unite, and London's ability to do the same is evident in its history, its streets, its sounds and its people.

That's what I found so appealing about the place when, as a teenager back in the 1970s, I began really listening to and appreciating music. So much of my favourite music stemmed from London. It was clearly a city of dreams and extremes, bright lights and excitement, all of which made it sound like an almost mythical city that was worlds away from the small market town of Bedford where I grew up. In contrast, Bedford's biggest claim to rock & roll fame occurred way back in 1963 when The Beatles played at the now demolished Granada cinema. And even then, they were apparently without John Lennon who was poorly that night.

But living just a quick fifty mile train journey north of the capital I was able to visit frequently and have loved doing so ever since. I particularly enjoyed people watching - as I still do to this day - a guilty pleasure that allowed me to remain anonymous as I happily watched the weird world go by. For although Bedford undoubtedly had its fair share of eccentric characters, they wouldn't have been worth even a second glance in London which seemed to be crammed full of cranks, crackpots, misfits and freaks, all living right on the edge. And while some hid it better than others, it felt as though nobody was ever more than a couple of steps away from falling off that cliff edge and into a complete frenzy. That ever-present sense of tension and exhilaration was totally lacking in my sleepy little home town where the most thrilling activity to be had was negotiating the one-way system that ensnares the town centre. But London's feisty attitude and taut atmosphere always provided me with that excitement, and the music that came out of the city encapsulated it perfectly.

London as a whole, or its individual boroughs, thoroughfares, parks and various locales have been mentioned in countless songs over the years, either as titles or in lyrics. In addition, numerous London scenes have featured in music videos or been photographed and used as album covers, some of which have become iconic, as have the many music venues that have helped to make it one of the most vibrant cities in the world.

For an idea of just how many songs feature London to some extent or other, try looking at Wikipedia's 'List of Songs about London'. There are so many it'll make your head hurt. Therefore, it would be impossible to acknowledge them all in this book, so I've chosen to feature a number of better known places that have had some of the most famous songs written about them, as well as celebrating many lesser known locations that may not be so familiar, but nevertheless have obscure and interesting backstories attached to them. In doing so, I hope to stir up some memories from the past and also help to better understand why decades of songwriters have found London so endearingly influential.

As is the case with most people, the music I loved through my teenage years and into my twenties is the music I still love today, because even as we get older the music from our past still has the power to shape our lives and influence our moods. When you hear an old favourite song you'll often feel a warm wave of nostalgia immediately wash over you and take you back to the place you first heard it. You'll be able to remember where you bought the record and where you listened to it, sometimes

Rock & Stroll

alone and sometimes with friends. Those friends may well have been chosen because they liked the same music as you. What we listened to often determined our fashion sense, our general appearance, our perception of others and sometimes even our life choices. It provided the soundtrack to our youth, ushered us into adulthood and made us who we are today. And even though it can occasionally take us back to a time or a place that was sometimes confusing and uncertain, we know it would never let us down. Like a trusted old friend, our music has always been there when we needed it, with strong words of advice, an affectionate memory or a loving hug. This book is my way of giving back some of that love.

I hope my journey around the streets of the capital will help you to see and hear songs you're already familiar with in a refreshingly different light, as well as possibly rediscovering some you've not heard in ages. It may also introduce you to some songs and artists you've never heard of before; I certainly found plenty. Most of the locations are fairly central too, so easy to walk between the next time you're out and about in London, with maybe an occasional bus or tube ride thrown in.

Well, what are you waiting for? It's time to start rocking & strolling, so get yourself an A to Z guidebook, find your way up the junction and stop being a Cockney rebel, because London's calling, and we need to get to Waterloo before sunset.

Rock & Stroll

Chapter 1
Spiritual Sunrise

There are many words that can be used to describe modern-day London: exhilarating, eccentric, exhausting, hectic, vibrant, chaotic, complex, bold, brash. But as I'm mapping out my walking tour around the streets of the capital, and most importantly where that journey should actually begin, there is one adjective that dominates all of my thoughts: big.

That one, daunting word. That one BIG word. And I have to work out a route on the map that's laid out in front of me. That one BIG map.

Obviously, while planning a project like this it's important that I should fit in as much content as I can. There are hundreds of musical references scattered all across inner London and through its outlying districts, but to visit them all would be an impossible task. So I've decided that my journey should include the most historic and most significant locations, while taking in many others en route that enable myself, and consequently you, dear reader, to experience the joy of making discoveries about music and about London. Therefore, I have already marked out the most notable of them on this map and it only takes a cursory glance to see that the majority of such places are predominantly fairly central. And as I've always believed that Central London itself is not as enormous as it appears at first glance, I make the decision to stay around the middle, confident that from there I can cover the bulk of the most relevant locations on foot.

Next I have to decide exactly where to start. I consider closing my eyes and sticking a pin into the map, but that is far too indiscriminate a way of managing a project to which I've already dedicated so much time. Not to mention the fact that significant areas of the map are now obscured by so many strategically applied streaks of black marker pen they've become almost indecipherable.

But the more I look and the more I think about it, the more certain I am that my journey should start at the location furthest to the north of the central cluster that I've marked on the map. That would mean starting at the top, which seems to be the natural place to begin. Good things nearly always start at the top, and from there you work your way down. That's why maps always have north at the top, because it's the closest point to the axis of rotation around which everything else revolves, and from there it's all heading south. It has to be north. Which means that it has to be Primrose Hill.

However, it's not just the grid reference that makes Primrose Hill the obvious choice. Its height, its history, its status and its significance to popular music means there can be no other option. So that's it, my mind is made up: period.

Happy to have finally made a decision, I can't wait to tell my friend Jacqui who has been very supportive of this venture, and I know she will agree that this is the perfect place to start. I've known Jacqui for a number of years, our daughters were friends at primary school and even though they've now grown up we have stayed in touch. We share a love of music, particularly from the 1970s and '80s, although she is far more open-minded to music from recent decades than I am. She grew up in North London herself and still heads down there whenever she can with her husband, David, and their daughter, Grace. They love the buzz of London and frequently make a long weekend of their visits, usually staying in Camden Town, their favourite part of the city.

*   *   *

"Why don't you start in Camden Town?" asks Jacqui, as I begin to outline my carefully considered plans.

"Ah, yes, Camden Town." I suppose I should have seen that one coming. "Well, I just think Primrose Hill is a more obvious place to start. It's a better fit for what I've got planned around the rest of the book."

"But there is so much music history surrounding Camden. It's so iconic; so vibey."

"Yes I know, but so is Primrose Hill," I respond, trying to sound decisive.

What a quandary. I have to admit I can see her point of view. Maybe I should have given it even more thought than I did. There is definitely a strong case for me to change my mind, but nonetheless I reiterate my initial intention. Whose book is this anyway?

"Don't worry, I'll still include some bits about Camden. Right after Primrose Hill."

"Okay," she concedes, with a heavy tone of disappointment. "So how will you get to Primrose Hill?"

Rock & Stroll

"I'll walk there from Camden Town tube station," I reply, immediately realising from the look on Jacqui's face that those few words had just lost me the debate.

Amid further discussions I admit to Jacqui that I'm not terribly well acquainted with Camden Town, having only visited at length a couple of times back in the 1990s at the height of Britpop, and even then my credentials as an urban trendy didn't quite cut the mustard. Since then it's left me even further behind and although I've passed through on odd occasions, I've never stayed for long, partly because it's always so crazily busy. Nonetheless, having been even further worn down by more chat about Camden, a few glasses of Merlot and a couple of tubes of Pringles, I am happy to admit that Jacqui is most probably right. It's obvious really, and with the two starting options being so close together geographically, it hardly even involves a change of plan.

* * *

And so it is that I find myself here on a Sunday morning in Camden Town, the area named in honour of prominent politician Charles Pratt, 1st Earl of Camden, who began leasing plots of land here in 1791 with a view to it becoming a major residential and commercial development. And modern-day Camden certainly proves the Earl's vision to have been very astute as it's nowadays dominated by a thriving mix of cafes, bars, markets and live music venues, all of which have helped it become one of the city's major centres of business, recreation and culture.

Rock & Stroll

Which does indeed make it the perfect place to begin my journey around London's greatest hits, although I'm afraid my introduction to the neighbourhood has seen my mood slightly dampened by a couple of rain showers and an early morning drunk hassling people at the exit from the tube station. Fortunately however, the rain has now stopped and the drunk has left me alone, but it's hardly the grand start I'd hoped for. Okay, I didn't expect marching bands and a firework display, but a bit of sunshine and a busker would have been nice.

Nonetheless, there is a definite bonus to starting from here as it allows me to begin my musical sightseeing tour immediately, as the tube station entrance featured in the video to Suggs' jolly reggae hit from 1995 that he titled 'Camden Town' after this, his favourite part of London. And very appropriately, this is also the starting point of the Camden Town Music Walk of Fame, a project which began in 2019 to celebrate the area's diverse musical heritage with a series of black and gold stone discs laid into the pavement. Madness, The Who, Amy Winehouse and Soul II Soul are among the early recipients of this honour, and as more famous names are added the walk is planned to extend the entire length of Camden High Street from Chalk Farm to Mornington Crescent.

Heading away from the tube station, north-westerly towards Chalk Farm, I ponder which artists could be added to the Walk of Fame in future. There are over 400 stones planned and numerous worthy candidates, mostly with connections to Camden itself, making this a fitting location for such a scheme. All of which will add further prestige to Camden Town's already hugely acclaimed status in the history of London's music scene, as it plays host to such places as The Roundhouse, Dingwalls, Dublin Castle, The Jazz Cafe and The Hawley Arms, to name just a few of its many clubs, pubs and dedicated concert venues. These have a history of showcasing a diversity of talent which have made Camden a centre of excellence for both firmly established and emerging artists, covering all genres of music.

It is particularly noted for its role in the punk revolution that occurred during the sizzling hot summer of 1976 when The Stranglers, The Clash, the Ramones and the Sex Pistols all played local gigs within a few days of each other. This made Camden mega cool and placed it firmly at the cutting edge of the latest music trends, resulting in the hippest original acts being attracted to play here in search of eager new followers. So much so that in 1983 even Madonna made her live UK debut at the now defunct Camden Palace, the venue subsequently being named Koko until it was badly damaged by a fire which caused it to close down in early 2020. Happily, it was repaired, refurbed and re-opened in early 2022 with a performance from the aptly named Canadian band Arcade Fire.

Carrying on down the High Street, it doesn't take long for me to pass one of Camden's most famous music venues, the Electric Ballroom. With a history dating back over eighty years it would be easier to list the acts that haven't performed or rehearsed here during that time, and despite London Underground having proposed several developments to the adjoining tube station that have threatened the Ballroom with demolition, it is thankfully still standing following a public enquiry and backing from several notable musicians. These included Bob Geldof,

Rock & Stroll

Boy George, Madness and Graham Coxon, and they may be needed again as Transport for London are still working on plans to develop the tube station that could finally pull the plug on the Electric Ballroom.

Considering it's still fairly early on this Sunday morning there's already quite a lot of activity on the High Street, proving that Jacqui was correct when she was selling Camden to me, as there certainly is an exciting vibe about the place. For even though it's relatively free from visitors at the moment, there is a real buzz building up as shopworkers, cafe owners and market stall holders scurry around, preparing themselves for business. Later on today, as with every day, this place will be absolutely heaving.

Running parallel to this stretch of Camden High Street is the more subdued Arlington Road, the site of a hostel and support centre for homeless people that once gave shelter to George Orwell. Although tucked away down this fairly anonymous side street, Arlington House has been referenced in songs by both The Pogues and Madness, the latter having featured it in the video to their 1984 hit 'One Better Day', much of which was filmed around Camden.

Madness themselves were formed in Camden during the mid-1970s and have always maintained very strong links with the area. In their early days they played many gigs around here, firstly as The Invaders and then later as Madness, a name change which further helped establish their reputation as a formidable live band. This was largely through their regular performances at the Dublin Castle on Parkway, a pub which also massively contributed to the impact of Britpop in the 1990s and in

Rock & Stroll

which local resident Amy Winehouse often used to perform as well.

A little further along the High Street and before I know it, I'm already approaching the focal point of Camden Lock, its name writ large in welcoming green and yellow on the side of the railway bridge that crosses the road, which in turn passes over the Regent's Canal - three contrasting transport systems from different ages, all layered one on top of the other.

The lock is a favourite meeting place for punk rockers who frequently congregate on the road bridge, giving an edgy vibe to the local culture. It's clearly far too early for them this morning though, as there are none present so far today. But I have to say that whenever I've seen them gathering around here, although their appearance is still outlandish they seem far nicer and much less threatening than the punks I remember from the 1970s, and more approachable too.

As well as the punks, this part of Camden is also a popular haunt for goths who regularly gather together to shop and display their individuality, all of which adds a nice splash of colour to the place - that colour, of course, being black.

Adjacent to Camden Lock itself is Dingwalls, another live concert hall that over the decades has staged performances from a wide range of artists including The Drifters, Elvis Costello, Red Hot Chili Peppers, R.E.M., Stereophonics, Ellie Goulding, Foo Fighters and George Ezra. In its early years, during the 1970s, it even hosted a gig by Kilburn and the High Roads, Ian Dury's band before he formed The Blockheads.

Rock & Stroll

Based around the old canal wharf are a collection of quirky markets that contribute so much to the flavour and spirit of the area, all made up of street stalls and outlets in converted warehouses. This entire market district is a marvellous cluster of commerce that cleverly blends the old, rustic, working class surroundings of canalside buildings and railway yards with the intoxicating energy of contemporary London.

The market stall holders are mostly independent traders, many of whom specialise in vintage and retro clothing, antique furniture, incense, trinkets and other artsy bric-a-brac, as well as grunge, punk and goth attire and accessories. But while the development of the markets has stayed true to the original architecture and nostalgic character of the place, the produce on sale at the food outlets is unashamedly modern and cosmopolitan. So instead of such age-old Cockney delicacies as jellied eels, cockles or pie and mash, you will now find street food representing all corners of the globe, from bagels, halloumi fries, felafel and tofu, to churros, sushi, frozen yoghurt and bubble tea.

Having lingered a while around Camden Lock I move on, passing under the railway bridge where Castlehaven Road veers off to the right and leads immediately to The Hawley Arms, another music venue whose voguish reputation was helped by its close proximity to the MTV studios. This led to many well known celebrities frequenting the place, with the likes of Liam Gallagher, Pete Doherty, Kate Moss and Amy Winehouse becoming regular customers, the latter having even been known to get behind the bar and pull pints when it got busy.

Rock & Stroll

After a short walk from the Hawley Arms I arrive at what is probably the most famous of all Camden's trading posts, the artistic and vibrant Stables Market. Sited around a former Victorian horse hospital, it is bordered by warehouses and cobbled yards where the air is always infused with a mouth-watering marinade of spices from the scores of canalside eateries and street food vendors who trade from here. It also features the brick alleyway in which The Clash were photographed for the cover of their debut album, most of which was rehearsed in the adjoining building. And nearby is a delightful bronze statue of Amy Winehouse, the undisputed Queen of Camden, which is so lifelike that as you stand looking at it all you can hear is her sultry, soulful voice laced with those distinctive dark jazz tones and powerful modern attitude singing to you. How fitting that she should be so stylishly immortalised in a place she loved so much.

These surroundings give the place a constant kaleidoscopic buzz that's as colourful, upbeat and vivacious as the mix of characters that flock here in numbers exceeding 25 million every year. And just as I'm leaving, I see my first punk of the day, a man that I'd guess is in his thirties, with a dyed red Mohican haircut, multiple tattoos and an abundance of facial piercings.

Moving away from the markets I venture further along Camden High Street, although I think I'm right in saying that it's now morphed into Chalk Farm Road. This stretch does seem to be much less indie and more mainstream as far as retail, restaurants and passers-by go, but even so I see a trendy young man cycling past on a Raleigh Chopper bike - lucky git, I always wanted one of those. Then, a little way ahead and to my left, I see the

Rock & Stroll

striking yellow brick rotunda of The Roundhouse, one of London's most famous live concert venues.

This imposing old railway building, which originally housed a turntable to rotate trains, opened as a music venue in 1966 with a show from Pink Floyd. The following years saw it host performances from numerous big names and influential acts such as David Bowie, the Rolling Stones, The Doors, Jimi Hendrix, Led Zeppelin, Otis Redding and Fleetwood Mac. Then, during the mid-1970s, it became hugely significant in the emergence of punk rock, having seen shows from The Clash, Patti Smith and the first UK gig from the Ramones. Over the decades it has also been used as the setting for many live concert recordings and video shoots.

Despite having undergone closure and redevelopment since its prime years, it is still a wonderfully stylish and impressive cutting edge performance venue, the interior being especially striking with a circular framework of cast iron pillars and struts supporting a high conical roof. It really is an amazing looking building, and with a history to match.

Almost immediately after The Roundhouse I bear left down Adelaide Road and pass Chalk Farm tube station, the front of which featured on 'Absolutely', the second album from Madness. Released in 1980 and featuring the hits 'Baggy Trousers' and 'Embarrassment', the album cover photo shows the band posing in fairly restrained fashion (for them anyway) against the oxblood red tiled backdrop of the station entrance.

Having then taken the first road on the left, I walk across the railway footbridge which takes me straight ahead into Regent's Park Road, just a short stroll from

Rock & Stroll

Primrose Hill, which will be the next stop on my hit parade. I am sorry to be leaving Camden Town behind, yet very happy to admit that Jacqui was most definitely right. How could I possibly have overlooked the importance of Camden Town? And why did it take so many Pringles to make me realise that my previous plan just wouldn't have done it justice?

*   *   *

Even though I am now only a few steps into the district of Primrose Hill, I can already sense that it has an altogether different and more restrained feel than Camden which enables it to remain relatively tranquil for such a busy place. I guess you could say it's the yin to Camden's yang.

As if to emphasise the difference I am immediately greeted by a range of fashionable restaurants, wine bars and shops that are more upmarket than I saw in Camden, along with a range of providers offering organic well-being products and services. I've also just seen a coffee shop with a board outside displaying its prices in that haughty way that many trendy cafes do nowadays, by omitting the final numeral from its price: Americano - 2.8, Earl Grey Tea - 2.4, Pain au Chocolat - 3.2. I don't know if they do this in order to appear less expensive or if it's to try and portray the image of a chic Parisian patisserie, but to leave out the last character just seems to me like a pretentious load of old bullshi.

Situated in NW3, Primrose Hill is an unashamedly prosperous residential area of pastel-hued Regency and Victorian terraces that can boast to have been home to many famous people over the years. The likes of broadcasters A.J.P. Taylor and Joan Bakewell, writers and poets W.B. Yeats, Dylan Thomas, Alan Bennett, Sylvia Plath and Ted Hughes, and even socialist revolutionary Friedrich Engels have all lived here. More recent residents, trendily known in the 1990s as the Primrose Hill Set, helped to keep the bohemian image alive. These included Kate Moss, Ewan McGregor, Sadie Frost and Jude Law, Noel and Liam Gallagher, and more recently Paddington Bear, with Chalcot Crescent being used in the films as his fictional home of Windsor Gardens.

Not surprisingly however, its most famous asset is the hill that's located on the north side of Regent's Park which gives its name to the surrounding district. Standing an impressive 80 metres above sea level, Primrose Hill towers above its immediate surroundings and is one of a handful of London's protected viewpoints, with surrounding trees kept low and building restricted to allow uninterrupted views over the city. Until the 19th century the hill was part of a wooded park within Middlesex Forest that contained large numbers of primroses and was regularly used as a hunting ground by British monarchs and sometimes even as a venue for fighting duels. In 1841 this whole area was bought from Eton College and became a Crown property, then shortly afterwards was designated as a public open space.

Its height also gives it strategic importance, making the summit a perfect spot for the Martians to have made their final encampment in H.G. Wells' 'War of the Worlds', and during World War II it was used as a site for anti-aircraft guns to repel the Luftwaffe. It also stages an annual Druid festival.

Rock & Stroll

So there is much history, as well as beautiful scenery, to inspire the many songs that have been written about Primrose Hill. In fact, of all the songs written about or featuring London landmarks, I can't think of any single location that has featured more.

These songs have been composed by the likes of Madness, Peggy Seeger, Saint Etienne and John and Beverley Martyn, whose wonderfully gentle number about watching the sun go down on Primrose Hill in 1970 was sampled by Fatboy Slim, aka Norman Cook, for his 2004 song 'North West Three'. While keeping true to the serenity of the original, this update gave the song a more modern, urban feel and a welcome revival for younger audiences to appreciate. More recently, indie-pop trio The Tailormade shot the video of their song that was written in honour of Primrose Hill on top of the hill itself, and this contributed to them being crowned in 2014 as 'Best Buskers in London' by then mayor Boris Johnson. I believe they're still doing okay though.

But surely the best known composition inspired by Primrose Hill has to be The Beatles' song 'The Fool on the Hill' which was written predominantly by Paul McCartney while he was living in London, as were all The Beatles at the height of their fame. Although the writing was credited to Lennon and McCartney on the disc, the idea for the song is said to have come to Paul following an incident one morning in 1967 while out walking his dog on the hill, when he suddenly encountered a strange lone man who looked bizarrely out of place. Having exchanged pleasantries, the smartly dressed stranger departed as swiftly and curiously as he had appeared, leaving Paul to wonder how he could have vanished so quickly and to speculate who he could have been.

Thirty years later Loudon Wainwright III, who lived for a time in nearby St John's Wood, also wrote a song about another mysterious local character that he'd seen on numerous occasions whilst cycling around the area. Sensing a back story, he did some asking around before eventually finding out that the man was in fact a former musician and busker who used to play on the underground before falling on hard times and falling out with society. Taking its title from the name of the hill, the song's lyrics make it clear that the man is homeless as they portray him drinking cans of beer from his sleeping bag of a home on the side of the hill, with just a guitar and his dog for company. To add an even greater sense of poignancy to this sad tale, Loudon Wainwright has also since discovered that the man has very sadly passed away.

Going back again to 1967, the Rolling Stones' album 'Between the Buttons' featured a shot of the band on its cover that was taken on Primrose Hill by British photographer Gered Mankowitz. It shows the band with trees in the background and was shot using a camera filter smeared with Vaseline to achieve the effect of the Stones dissolving into their surroundings, but made it so blurry that, to be honest, it could have been taken pretty much anywhere.

But now, as I stand on Regent's Park Road having never visited Primrose Hill before, it's the marvellously tranquil song by John and Beverley Martyn, and particularly its sultry saxophone riff, that is running round my head as I look up at this lush green landmark. The hill is positively humming with the sound of music making the climb to the top an enticing prospect, yet also quite daunting as it's a fair bit higher than I was expecting. But it's now quite a pleasant morning, the sun is trying to peep through and that bit of rain that fell earlier has filled the air with a fragrant petrichor (Google it - I had to). There are already a dozen or so people visible at the top and small children running around the network of paths and jumping about like hot popcorn, so if they can manage it, then dammit, I'm sure I can make that climb to see what it was that inspired McCartney.

  I commence briskly with purposeful strides, but my early keenness begins to wane as the incline steepens and the going starts to get tough. To be honest, I thought I was in better shape than this. When I was younger it would have been a doddle climbing up here, but now I'm in my late fifties I'm more prone to sciatic tensing than well-honed like Sherpa Tenzing. I press on though, as a young child hurtles down the path towards me, just about managing to keep his feet enough to avoid face-planting into the tarmac. These kids have no fear.

  Nearing the top, the sun very kindly breaks through the remaining few clouds and the refreshing breeze intensifies to blow away all my cobwebs. On a windy day I suspect it would blow away a lot more besides. Then, finally, I reach the summit, quite breathless but elated at the sight that greets me - one of the greatest cities in the world laid out before me in all its splendour. You can see for miles and the view is so stunning it's no wonder scores of artists and writers of song and verse have felt moved to create from this spot. It's a place to marvel at what this fine city has to offer, yet is high enough and far enough away from its frenetic pace to feel somewhat detached

Rock & Stroll

from it. I guess that's why Amy Winehouse often visited this hilltop, for a chance to clear her head and escape from the perplexities of stardom.

Dominating the foreground is the BT tower which is illuminated against a backdrop of other magnificent structures: The Houses of Parliament and Big Ben, The London Eye, St Paul's Cathedral, Westminster Cathedral, The Shard, The Gherkin, Canary Wharf Tower, and ever so much more. This spectacular mix of ancient and modern can't fail to inspire and really is one of the best ways to view many of London's most famous landmarks - albeit from quite a distance - even though Prince Charles might not be so keen on some examples of the more contemporary architecture.

It's fascinating trying to identify the buildings that I can't immediately recognise, as well as looking further afield to see if I can spot any landmarks on the horizon, which fades to a distant grey and seems quite insignificant compared to the impressive scenery that stretches out before it. Like Paul McCartney's fool on the hill, I stand here for ages with my head in the clouds, so lost in my reverie that I don't even notice a young girl of about nine-years-old standing right in front of me, until she says sorry for getting in the way. As if she could possibly spoil such a marvellous view, but it was sweet of her to apologise and I tell her all is fine.

I had seriously considered wearing AirPods during my travels so that I could listen to the music that related to each of the locations I visited, but being a bit old fashioned I decided not to bother. Now I'm here it's a relief to say that I made the right decision as it clearly wouldn't have worked for me. I'm sure that a lot of people would have done so, and I certainly wouldn't blame them because I have to admit that in some ways it would be nice to hear songs about Primrose Hill while standing on top of it. The downside however, is that wearing ear phones would have prevented me from fully appreciating views such as this and being able to experience the true atmosphere of the places that I visit, hence reducing the adventure to a level close to that of mundane everyday travel.

Time passes so quickly up here that before I know it, I've already spent ages absorbing the sights from the well maintained viewing area which is bordered by a stone edging beautifully inscribed with a quote from another former resident of the area, 18th century painter and romantic poet William Blake:

"I have conversed with the spiritual Sun. I saw him on Primrose Hill."

It's a simple quote, yet one that perfectly reflects the uplifting nature of the view as standing this high certainly does give the feeling of being closer to the sun, which is now shining bright. This timely gesture of reverence to the city also casts shimmering rays of light far away into the distance, creating an ethereal glow that makes it all feel quite unworldly.

Billy Bragg, the Bard of Barking, salutes William Blake in his song 'Upfield', which tells of a man climbing high on Primrose Hill in search of some peace away from the busy streets. Once there he sees angels in the trees (a reference to Blake's many angelic visions) and they fly with him over some of the misery and deprivation that abounds within the city. The man is deeply affected by this spiritual encounter and enlightened to take socialism into his heart. It's a lively, uplifting song that features on the

Rock & Stroll

1996 album entitled 'William Bloke', further proof that Billy Bragg is clearly a huge fan of Blake.

Having climbed a mountain and enjoyed the view for long enough to feel the early onset of altitude sickness, I now hurry down the hill, I guess in much the same way the Red Hot Chili Peppers did in their 1999 song 'Emit Remmus' (Summer Time spelt backwards) before they carried on to Leicester Square, just as I eventually intend to do myself.

As I continue my descent I admire the casual, if slightly outdated, dress sense of a middle-aged man sauntering towards me in a baggy white linen shirt, faded calf length jeans and white espadrilles. Or maybe that's all coming back into fashion? Either way, he looks like a refugee from Duran Duran.

To my left is the quirky, origami-like structure of London Zoo's aviary and Regent's Park, which provides the title for an equally quirky composition by British singer-songwriter Bruno Major. Released in 2020, this beautiful song of heartbreak is made even more poignant and enchanting as it samples a song called 'A Beautiful Spring Day' composed by George Bruns. This number features in the Disney film '101 Dalmations', where it plays over the scene in which Pongo first meets Perdita while taking walkies in Regent's Park. What a great example of two lovely songs from very different times and genres merging seamlessly into one.

While I've thoroughly enjoyed my first visit to Primrose Hill and been moved by the William Blake quote engraved at the summit, I must confess to feeling a little disappointed that there no longer appears to be any trace of another famous inscription that used to adorn the hill.

Rock & Stroll

Painted in white on one of the pathways, it featured the lyric "and the view's so nice" which was taken from Blur's 1993 song 'For Tomorrow' and was apparently laid out by a couple of local residents using paint left over from decorating their flat. This piece of handiwork proved to be very popular with locals and tourists alike, especially as the song mentions Primrose Hill and the video, shot in various locations around London, features the band flying kites on top of the hill as Damon Albarn rolls down it. Over time however, the inscription gradually wore away, allegedly with help from The Royal Parks, the body charged with managing much of London's parkland.

It was repainted in 2012 by local enthusiasts but sadly didn't last long as The Royal Parks were again suspected of having intervened with a bottle of paint stripper which, if true, I suppose is proof that one person's art is another person's graffiti.

On my way along the path towards St Edmunds Terrace I see a dog - I think it's a cockapoo - being chased by a butterfly. Its owners, a young American sounding couple, are oblivious to its plight as they stand over an empty bird's nest on the grass, debating how it could possibly have got there. I glance up at the tree they're standing beneath but resist the temptation to introduce them to the concept of gravity.

Having finally left Primrose Hill, I progress along St Edmunds Terrace onto the ambiguously titled Avenue Road before then turning left into Acacia Road. Along here I cross the intriguingly named Woronzow Road which, during later research, I discover is dedicated to Count Simon Woronzow, Russian ambassador to the United Kingdom from 1784-1806, who lived in

Rock & Stroll

Marylebone. Upon his death in 1832 he left a bequest to the poor of the parish, a philanthropic act that led to the building of the St Marylebone Almshouses that are still standing to this today.

Further along I pass St John's Wood tube station which, as any saddo with an obsession for useless bits of trivia that might one day crop up in a pub quiz will tell you (yes, I'm talking about me), is the only station on the underground network not to share any letters with the word "mackerel".

I then cross Finchley Road to head down Grove End Road, and there is a certain something in the air that makes me feel a growing sense of anticipation; a sense that I am about to experience an event that could change my life. Maybe it's due to the opulent Georgian grandeur of the properties that line this particular street, or the numerous blue plaques marking the houses of previous residents, including that of the conductor and impresario Sir Thomas Beecham. My levels of expectation continue to rise at the amount of Ferraris and Aston Martins that I can see, either gliding past or parked behind firmly locked gated entrances. There is some serious money around here.

The excitement increases still further as I hurry on, now getting closer to the sound of nearby car horns and a general hubbub of people gathering just ahead of me down the street. There's definitely something brewing, and whatever it is, it sounds like it's going to be big.

Finally, upon reaching the end of the road, I look expectantly to my right and at last I can see exactly what all this commotion has been about.

A zebra crossing.

Chapter 2
Zebragate

The Swinging Sixties are often credited as being the defining period of 20th century Britain. A time of excitement, freedom and hedonism, where suddenly everything was in glorious Technicolor after years of drab austerity. And yet a photograph of something as ordinary as a zebra crossing was still able to become one of the most celebrated images of the decade.

The cultural and historical importance of this piece of street furniture is, of course, due to the fact that the people using it to walk across the road just happened to be The Beatles, and that the photograph adorned one of their best-loved albums: 'Abbey Road'.

Situated within the tree-lined affluence of St John's Wood, Abbey Road, which was constructed in 1829 and named due to its close proximity to Kilburn Abbey, already had a claim to fame, being the site of the world's first purpose built recording studio.

Opened by EMI in 1931 with an inaugural performance of 'Land of Hope and Glory' by Sir Edward Elgar, this converted nine-bedroom villa went on to become one of the most famous buildings on the planet. During its time as a studio it has been responsible for numerous important recordings of historic events, such as

Rock & Stroll

Russian composer Sergei Prokofiev's first ever recording, Glenn Miller's last ever recording, and capturing the sound of the coronation of King George VI and his famous "King's Speech" at the outbreak of World War II. And from those early years it has proved itself to be at the cutting edge of recording technology, through the production of countless pieces of music from all genres, be it classical, rock or movie scores, ensuring that Abbey Road Studios is still revered as one of the most significant and influential music locations in the world. But it was during the late 1950s and early 1960s that it first really established itself as being *the* place for rock & roll.

    Cliff Richard started that particular ball rolling when he recorded 'Move It' here in 1958, a number generally regarded as being one of the first genuine rock & roll songs to be produced outside the USA. Four years later The Beatles also recorded their first single, 'Love Me Do', at Abbey Road and followed that by recording 190 of their 210 songs at the studios. A solo John Lennon recorded 'Imagine' here, Cliff and The Shadows did 'Summer Holiday', Pink Floyd did 'Dark Side of the Moon' and Kate Bush recorded 'Never For Ever', while also mentioning the studio in her song 'Moments of Pleasure'. Bearing in mind its relevance to the history of music, it's surprising Abbey Road Studios hasn't featured in the lyrics to more songs.

    A plethora of other great artists, including Stevie Wonder, Michael Jackson, Queen, Oasis, Amy Winehouse, Kanye West, Ed Sheeran, Radiohead, Adele and, in fact, anyone else who's anybody, have all recorded here. But it's the album that bears its photograph (the name Abbey Road

Rock & Stroll

doesn't actually appear on the original sleeve) that has cemented its place in the cultural heritage of Great Britain.

Produced by the legendary George Martin, the 'Abbey Road' album was released in 1969 and contained such classic songs as 'Come Together', 'Something', 'Golden Slumbers', 'Here Comes the Sun' and 'Maxwell's Silver Hammer'. As the last Beatles disc to be recorded ('Let It Be' was released a year later to coincide with the film, but had in fact been recorded earlier), this would always be a landmark album. But over time, Iain Macmillan's cover photo of the Fab Four walking over the zebra crossing away from the studio, the direction of travel signifying the end of the group's recording career, has become as well known as any of their songs.

Taken on the 8th August 1969 during a 10 minute window provided by a policeman halting the traffic, it is a wonderfully simple image that juxtaposes four of the most famous people on the planet against something so mundanely British as a zebra crossing. The fifth Beetle (sic) in the photo, the white Volkswagen on the left just behind George Harrison's head, also became famous despite only having a supporting role. Owned by a resident from a local block of flats, it just happened to be parked there on the day of the shoot, a serendipitous piece of photobombing that adds hugely to the overall perspective of the photograph and made such a star of the car that the registration plate (LMW 281F) was stolen many times. Its appearance in the photo also worked wonders for the long-term popularity of the VW Type-1, to give the car its official title, and it is now happily retired and on display at the Volkswagen museum in Wolfsberg, Germany.

Rock & Stroll

The zebra crossing too, is now so synonymous with The Beatles that in 2010 it was granted Grade 2 listed status by British Heritage and is unsurprisingly the only pedestrian crossing to hold such an honour. And being a site of historical interest and national importance it is a popular destination for visitors to the capital, although some people clearly want the moon on a stick as several comments on Tripadvisor are less than complimentary, opining that "it really is just a zebra crossing" and that "the traffic ruined it." Not sure what else they could have realistically been expecting, but most visits do appear to be overwhelmingly positive, particularly from Japanese tourists, a sign of just how massive The Beatles continue to be in Japan.

This popularity dates back to their appearances at the celebrated Tokyo Budokan in 1966 where they played five concerts, some of which were televised, making them one of the first, and certainly the biggest, band to perform in the Land of the Rising Sun. This came at a time when Japan, like the United Kingdom, were still redefining themselves after the war, and while many traditionalists opposed the concerts they were hugely successful and symbolic.

Standing outside Abbey Road Studios today, I get a true sense of just how much The Beatles are adored in Japan as their exuberant tourists clearly outnumber other nationalities by a sizeable amount. Among them is a very excited and brightly dressed lady who proudly announces to her fellow Japanese companions that the sight of the zebra crossing has just made her "feel like a goosepimp," which I assume is a mispronunciation of goosepimples rather than a declaration of some weird avian perversion.

Rock & Stroll

However, as I watch the goings-on at this monument to Beatlemania, the downside to all its popularity is immediately apparent. There are masses of predominantly Japanese and American tourists causing never-ending chaos as they stroll over the crossing, imitating the strides of their heroes and then pausing for photos while traffic builds around them. No sooner does one foursome leave the crossing than another steps on, not in the slightest bit concerned at the frustration they're causing, presumably under the misapprehension that a middle-fingered gesture delivered by a snarling van driver is just cheerful Cockney banter. Then they generally respond by waving cheerily back, which only serves to further aggravate the situation.

Happily, all the fun and frolics of this unintended Beatles legacy are available to view online with a 24-hour live webcam if you'd care to grab yourself a beer and watch it all from the comfort of your own armchair. But I have to say it's far more entertaining to witness it in person, and not just to see white van man getting hacked off. It's quite a moving experience to stand at this iconic setting by the zebra crossing, which is instantly recognisable from the album cover, and outside number 3 Abbey Road, which is still a busy recording studio. As such, it is not open for tours but has a gift shop next door selling mainly Beatles memorabilia, ranging from tea towels to t-shirts, key rings to cufflinks and enough yellow submarines to sink a battleship. Other local souvenirs that are not so readily available are the Abbey Road street name signs that are noticeably mounted very high up on the walls of buildings so as to prevent them from being stolen, even though people still try. And outside the studio there is also a graffiti wall that fills up so quickly with messages of love for The Beatles that it has to be cleaned frequently.

While the photo on 'Abbey Road' makes it possibly the most famous album cover ever, it has also led to two great conspiracy theories. Firstly, shortly after the album's release there was much debate about the significance of the band's attire, particularly Paul McCartney's lack of footwear. The conspiracy theory proposed not that his feet were too hot, as he has himself since disclosed, but that he'd been tragically killed in a car crash in 1966 and so had to be replaced by a lookalike. This theory, which was originally attributed to a journalism student from America (where else?), was apparently confirmed by John being dressed in white (a priest), Ringo in black (a mourner) and George in denim (a gravedigger), along with many other vague clues and tenuous references in song lyrics and photos. This belief remains widespread amongst conspiracy theorists to this day despite many bigger clues to the contrary, such as Macca appearing live at every charity gig and national celebration ever since. McCartney even poked fun at these hoax stories himself on his 1993 album 'Paul Is Live', both with the album title and on the cover, which shows a picture of him walking on the crossing, wearing shoes, superimposed onto the original photograph.

The second theory has to do with the location of the crossing. In the mid 1990s, a sadly missed friend of mine, John Coughlan, then a resident of nearby Swiss Cottage, told me the zebra crossing had in fact been moved and was now several metres from the original, so that all these unfortunate tourists were not in fact walking in the footsteps of their idols. We both found this very funny, particularly John who had a very acerbic, no holds barred wit. He always reminded me of Bernie Taupin, Elton John's lyricist, both in his appearance and raconteur style of conversation, and we agreed that this mix up over the zebra crossing would also have appealed greatly to John Lennon's wry sense of humour.

For years I believed the crossing had moved, but I've recently discovered this might not be the case. It appears likely the rumour may have been started by local residents in an attempt to dissuade tourists from visiting the crossing. Many people have sought to establish the truth behind the scandal by studying current photos of the area against the original Iain Macmillan shot, comparing such things as marks on the pavement and fire hydrant covers, then taking into account shadows, camera angles and foreshortening, and yet are still none the wiser. This is not helped by Westminster City Council remaining tight-lipped despite attempts to get them to confirm or deny the rumour, presumably as they also see the confusion as a useful, if somewhat lax, aid to traffic management.

So I guess you pay your money and take your choice in the matter. If you can't bear the thought of such a historic landmark being moved, then you will be a fervent remainer. But if you favour the sardonic over the iconic, you will no doubt be delighted at the thought of thousands of tourists being conned into posting joyful Facebook and Instagram photos of themselves crossing a fairly ordinary piece of road. And if that's your preference, you would probably also be interested in visiting Abbey Road station on the Docklands Light Railway, situated in the East End many miles away from the recording studio, but which frequently receives visits from bewildered tourists searching for anything that looks remotely like a zebra crossing. I think that might have amused John Lennon too.

The debate about the possible relocation of the crossing provided London based rock band Shriekback (formed by Barry Andrews and Dave Allen, formerly of XTC and Gang of Four respectively), with the inspiration for a song called 'Beatles Zebra Crossing?' which featured on their 1992 album 'Sacred City'. This song again throws into question the special nature of the crossing, asking whether or not it is the original, yet still fails to provide a definite answer. Maybe that's part of the magic, that people think it probably is, but just can't be 100% certain.

But if the story about the crossing being moved is nothing more than a piece of fiction designed to keep tourists off the road, it clearly hasn't worked. Because although it may not be the original, it's still close enough and is well worth visiting, even if just to see how much it means to people from all over the world.

Having watched all the activity around the studios for a lengthy amount of time, I now walk off towards Maida Vale, my next destination and also the location of another famous music studio. Before leaving however, I consider strolling over the crossing myself, feeling especially tempted to halt the progress of a Lamborghini as it comes roaring into view. But as I've never been one to follow the crowd I decide it's probably better watching from the cheap seats anyway, so I wander off and cross further up the street, just by the strikingly beautiful Abbey Road Baptist Church, and without the aid of a zebra crossing. To be honest, it's not that much of a busy road anyway and would presumably have been even less so

Rock & Stroll

back in the 1960s, so it's a bit difficult to understand why they felt the need for a pedestrian crossing at all. In fact, the only problem with traffic volume and congestion along here seems to be caused solely by the existence of this particular zebra crossing, weirdly making it a victim of its own success.

At the point of departing Abbey Road I pause for a last look back towards the chaos this interactive music attraction is still causing outside the studios, and just in time to see a fairly hefty quartet of baseball-capped American tourists step onto the crossing and come together with the traffic. Despite now being a fair distance away I can still hear a cacophony of car horns as the not so Fab Four pause for photos halfway across the road, and one of the American men shouting at a taxi driver to "Stop kvetching!". This has no calming effect on the irate cabbie whatsoever, but it's a great word and so I make a mental note to slip it into conversation myself the next time I get half a chance.

Then, as I turn left into Abercorn Place to finally leave all this behind, I smile at how much fun the faithful are having keeping The Beatles' legacy alive for future generations to enjoy this set of road markings that are steeped in history and shrouded in mystery. And then I smile even more, in grateful thanks that I don't have to drive through it every day.

Rock & Stroll

Chapter 3
Anthem for Doomed Yoof

Abercorn Place continues the theme of fashionably upmarket residential streets in this part of North West London with numerous large mansions, many of which appear to be divided into studio flats, all spaciously laid out along its edges. Several streets around here have notices announcing the presence of private security patrols and they are certainly visible. This is clearly a millionaire's manor that can boast some magnificent properties.

    About halfway along Abercorn Place is Violet Hill, a narrower, more compact street that again boasts some very desirable, if generally smaller abodes and which lends its name to a 2008 song by Coldplay. Released as the lead single from their album 'Viva la Vida', 'Violet Hill' is a mournful anti-war song that is quite Beatlesque in its sound, which is entirely appropriate given the street's close proximity to Abbey Road. It tells the story of a reluctant soldier visiting Violet Hill with his lover, and he talks to her of how times are changing through the dark Decembers of war, of banks becoming cathedrals and of priests with rifles, while she remains silent as they sit in the snow, presumably in the quaint public gardens at the end of the street.

The park itself is a small but highly attractive haven with colourful flowers, shrubs and a play area for young children, all hidden away in the shadow of St Mark's Church impressive steeple. From the memorial plaques on the benches around the perimeter it is clear this charming little refuge of serenity means a great deal to many families and as such is a very apt setting for an anti-war anthem.

It is one of Coldplay's most popular songs, although I have to wonder quite how the members of the band could have discovered the park given that it's pretty tricky to find, hidden well away in a quiet little corner where Violet Hill meets Abbey Gardens. I can only guess that one day while out walking, possibly taking a break from recording at Abbey Road Studios, Chris Martin may have decided, like me, to pop into the park to make use of their public convenience. And very convenient it is too, as I was starting to become quite concerned as to when I would find a toilet. How can a city that has so many places selling liquid beverages still have so few places to take a leak?

Although 'Violet Hill' is a nice enough song, I have to confess that I'm not really a fan of Coldplay - there, I've said it. It's not that I have anything against them per se, and I certainly don't wish to disparage one of the biggest supergroups in the world. Indeed, every time I've seen any of the band interviewed they always come across as very likeable people and I applaud their philanthropic works and eco credentials, but I'm afraid their music just doesn't appeal to me. Believe me, I have tried, but I find it relies too heavily on the anthemic style of soft stadium rock and is too tame for my taste. However, bearing in mind the multi-million fan base they have, I'm sure they can happily carry on writing as many rock anthems as they like without caring one jot whether or not I like them.

Having enjoyed the ambience, as well as the facilities, of Violet Hill, I feel quite thankful to be leaving the park just in time to avoid having the experience ruined by a millennial man trying in vain, and very loudly, to control his two sons, Eefan and Nayfan. Presumably that's not how the names are spelt on their birth certificates, but I guess he didn't consider his inability to make a "th" sound to be particularly crucial when it came to pronouncing the names of his own children.

I return to Abercorn Place and continue along to the junction with Maida Vale where, as I begin to cross this busy intersection, I gasp loudly as a cyclist races through a red traffic light and very narrowly misses striking a young female pedestrian. I look around to see the reactions of other onlookers before realising that no-one else has even batted an eyelid, least of all the pedestrian herself, despite very nearly being flattened. Presumably this is such a common occurrence it's only an out-of-towner like me that would take any notice.

The unusually named Maida Vale is so called due to its proximity to a local pub which commemorated a British victory over the French at the Battle of Maida during the Napoleonic wars. It is a wide, mainly residential thoroughfare lined with trees and blocks of mansion flats - so yet another fancy-pants posh part of London that I'll never be able to afford to live in, unless this book sells a lot better than I'm hoping (it's reasonably

Rock & Stroll

priced and easy to wrap for the perfect Christmas present). As it progresses south it becomes Edgware Road before reaching the canal moorings at Paddington Basin, where the Regent's Canal meets the Paddington Arm of the Grand Union Canal to form the picturesque junction known as Little Venice.

Maida Vale also gives its name to the surrounding district which itself is synonymous with live music, being home to the world renowned studios in Delaware Road, one of the BBC's earliest premises. Comprised of seven sound studios, it was first used for broadcasting music in the early 1930s but is undoubtedly now most famous for staging John Peel's Radio One Live Sessions. These have seen many of the world's biggest pop stars perform there while some, such as The Beatles, David Bowie and Nirvana, have released albums featuring their live BBC performances.

London born singer-songwriter Linda Hoyle also included a song called 'Maida Vale' on her 2015 album 'The Fetch', her first solo release for over 40 years. It's a splendidly atmospheric narrative song that recalls her time spent working and recording in the area as a member of progressive jazz-rock group Affinity in the late 1960s. The lyrics vividly tell the story of performing in smoke filled pubs, of music contracts, two-track tapes, black and white TV, indiscretions at Oddbins and of minding the gap on the Bakerloo Line, all of which is richly evocative of that period in time.

Affinity only lasted four years, from 1968 to 1972, following which Linda Hoyle worked extensively as an art therapist, and while her song doesn't paint her time with the band as a particularly glamorous one, she sings it with such emotive poignancy that you feel as though you experienced it all with her.

A little way passed Maida Vale tube station (interestingly, the first station to be staffed entirely by women, having opened during World War I), I divert up Randolph Avenue to Paddington Recreation Ground, which this morning is being very well used. There are children frolicking in the large adventure playground and a variety of sports being played, from boxing and basketball to athletics, tennis and football, none of which has anything to do with music but it's nevertheless well worth visiting for the park's historic sporting connections. For on the wall of the very smart pavilion, there are two blue plaques, one of which is dedicated to Sir Roger Bannister who, while studying at nearby St Mary's Medical School, trained on the athletic track in preparation for running the first sub-four minute mile, in 1954. The other plaque celebrates Sir Bradley Wiggins who lived and attended school nearby, and while doing so got in some early training towards winning an Olympic gold medal and the Tour de France by cycling round his local rec. To think that these great sporting exploits could have been achieved from such humble beginnings as a public park makes you feel proud to be British.

Sadly, as I leave the recreation ground and head down Biddulph Road, that feeling of pride is challenged by some child-like scrawl on the side of an industrial sized wheelie bin that reads "Good Save The Queen." Young people today, huh? If you're going to graffiti something, then for good's sake make sure you spell it right. Assuming, of course, it is a spelling mistake and not a comment on Her Majesty's ability as a goalkeeper, then it's a poor reflection on modern-day youth that they can't even correctly spell the name of their own national anthem.

I know it shouldn't really bother me, maybe I'm just at that funny age where I've become a grumpy old curmudgeon (no need to answer that), but thankfully I'm over it by the time I've made my way to Elgin Avenue, a lengthy street which runs down to the Harrow Road and features in a number of songs.

The Tom Robinson Band recorded a live song called 'Elgin Avenue' during a 1978 gig in San Francisco, which then seemed to be largely forgotten until being released much later as a very popular additional track on the 2004 remastered version of their 'TRB Two' album. The esteemed Rick Wakeman also recorded the classical piano instrumental 'Elgin Mansions' on his 1985 solo album 'Silent Nights', a piece which alluded to one of three residential blocks built on Elgin Avenue in the early 1900s. And before joining The Clash, Joe Strummer was in a pub rock outfit called The 101ers, that name having derived from a squat some of the band lived in at 101 Walterton Road, Maida Vale. In the mid 1970s they also recorded a compilation album called 'Elgin Avenue Breakdown' that was eventually released in the early 1980s on the back of the success achieved by The Clash.

As I stroll away from Elgin Avenue to my next destination, I side-step three jolly guys to allow them to pass by without breaking ranks and observe that each one of them is sporting a hipster beard at various stages of germination. With the amount of beards around nowadays I can't help thinking that the government could take a leaf out of Tsar Peter the Great's book and introduce a beard

Rock & Stroll

tax. It could overturn the nation's spending deficit in a week.

Continuing towards the Paddington end of the Maida Vale district, I pause while walking down Warrington Crescent to look at the blue plaque mounted on the wall of number 2, a building that is nowadays a hotel but which has a proud historic boast. For this marks the birthplace of the incredible Alan Turing, World War II codebreaker and a man acknowledged as one of the founding fathers of modern computer science. It really is quite a humbling experience to see the childhood home of such a great man, and as I stand here looking at the front of the house I try to visualise him in my mind. I can see him as a smartly dressed and energetic young boy, fascinated by the world around him as he excitedly hurries up the steps that lead to the front door, eager to tackle his next adventure or make his next discovery. Ironically, this picture I have of him is one of the very few people I've seen today who is not interacting with some form of computer in one way or another.

From Warrington Crescent I emerge onto Warwick Avenue and am momentarily whisked back to my own childhood as I pass an elderly gent standing on the corner while enjoying smoking his pipe. I can't recall having smelled pipe tobacco for decades but as he puffs out a cloud of smoke, the sweetly pungent aroma so distinctly takes me back all those years that I have to quickly check I'm not wearing hand-me-down sandals and short trousers.

Reassured that I am suitably dressed for my age, I make my way towards the Transport for London roundel sign that marks the entrance to Warwick Avenue underground station, the place that gave Duffy the idea for her mega hit in 2008. Inspired to write the song shortly after relocating to London from her native North Wales, the young Aimee Anne Duffy passed through Warwick Avenue tube station one day while taking a train on the Bakerloo Line. The name of the station struck a chord with her as an Average Joe kind of place that would make a good title for a song, but there was nothing average about the lyrics that followed as she co-wrote and recorded the track for her hugely successful debut album, 'Rockferry'.

Although it may sound like a fairly run-of-the-mill sort of place, the location of the tube station at the junction of Warwick Avenue and Clifton Gardens is actually very attractive and would have tourist appeal as a scene on a picture postcard. Set in a broad, spacious boulevard of predominantly icing sugar white town houses, it is overlooked by the needle-sharp fibreglass spire of the modern St Saviour's Church which itself featured in the video for The Human League's 1981 hit 'Love Action (I believe in Love)'. The entrance to the underground station is also undeniably quaint, with its dark green iron railings painted to colour match the cabbie's shelter which stands in the middle of the junction, one of the few still operating in the capital.

These wooden shelters were instigated in the late 19th century by a group of philanthropists led by The Globe newspaper editor George Armstrong, and including the Earl of Shaftesbury, in order to give Hansom cab drivers somewhere to congregate for shelter and refreshment. At one time there were more than sixty of these shed-like shelters being frequented by taxi drivers all over London but now only thirteen remain, and as places of historic interest they are protected as Grade 2 listed buildings.

While you have to be a licensed cabbie to enter a shelter for refreshments, some of these surviving shelters do sell snacks to the public through a serving hatch and I have heard rumours that a certain local resident, namely Paul Weller, has been known to visit the Warwick Avenue shelter for a spot of breakfast. How rock and roll!! Unfortunately though, it's closed on Sundays so there's no chance of us sharing a cup of coffee here today.

It would be great to think that Duffy might once have stopped by too, possibly even while filming the video to the song which made the station famous. It shows her being driven away from Warwick Avenue station in the back of a black cab, all teary-eyed as she sings about the break-up of a relationship. It's an intensely moving film, the song being performed with a tough vulnerability made even more heartbreaking by the stark simplicity of the video in which she cries real tears, and is a great example of music and visuals combining to powerful yet sublime effect.

One consequence of the song however, is that Warwick Avenue, a hitherto fairly anonymous underground station, has now become a metaphor for failed relationships. And with that sombre thought in mind, I finally bid farewell to this swanky part of North West London and continue trekking towards my next destination of Baker Street. It's only about a twenty minute walk away, so not too taxing for a man of my age and degree of fitness, and also a great opportunity to burn off some calories.

Or else I could just take the tube.

Rock & Stroll

Chapter 4
Juke Box Fury

When you alight from the train onto the platform at Baker Street tube station you are immediately aware that the place has a special aura surrounding it. You can feel a certain sense of history, which is not surprising since it opened way back in 1863 and as such was one of the world's first underground railway stations. It then quickly gained further importance as the gateway to Central London from the developing outlying suburbs which came to be popularly known as Metroland.

It also has huge literary significance which is evident from some elementary detective work, as you don't need to be Sherlock Holmes to deduce that Baker Street used to be the dwelling place of, well, Sherlock Holmes. There are clues all around as the station seems to be almost entirely dedicated to him. The tiling on the walls of the Jubilee Line platform depicts in silhouette his pipe-smoking, deerstalkered, popular image; the Circle Line platform features decorative wooden architecture that I doubt has changed much since Sherlock's time as it has more than a hint of Victorian penny dreadful about it; there are several prominent signs advertising the nearby Sherlock Holmes Museum, and as you leave the station by the Marylebone Road exit there is a nine-feet high statue of him, again in very recognisable pose and attire; then, from there, you can take the brightly coloured 'Wonderpass' under the main road, the walls of which are again adorned with images and info about the man.

But if Sir Arthur Conan Doyle's detective creation has cornered the literary market around these parts, the musical prize undoubtedly goes to Gerry Rafferty for his Ivor Novello Award winning song which has become one of the most famous and enduring songs ever written about London. It is a true classic.

Rafferty's 'Baker Street' was released in February 1978 and was a massive success around the world. It also has special significance for me personally because that was the first year that I really started listening to music seriously, and so it became the soundtrack to my summer. As such it defines not just the street but also a hugely important time in my life, which contributed largely to my youthful and ongoing fascination with London.

The record, which debuted as the first single from the album 'City to City', is about as close to perfection as you can get in a rock song. Musically and lyrically it creates an intense atmosphere that's so skilfully crafted around a melancholic storyline it still sends shivers down my spine to this day, just as it did all those years ago. It tells of being down and depressed in a soulless city, of being stuck in a tired rut and desperately wanting to escape the situation. I can imagine that's a common issue in London because even though I love visiting the place, I have often wondered how on earth people manage to live here. It's brilliant for a few days out, but I bet that sense of excitement can very soon disappear when you experience it every single day.

Rock & Stroll

Although written in the second person, that feeling of being trapped probably felt very personal to Gerry Rafferty because, at the time, he was trying to extricate himself from a recording contract agreed while still a member of his previous band, Stealers Wheel. During this period of legal wrangling he regularly visited a friend who had a flat in Baker Street and they would seek mutual solace in the bottom of a glass. Hence, Baker Street was strongly symbolic of his frustrations as well as his hopes of release.

Tragically, Gerry Rafferty passed away from liver failure in 2011, but in 'Baker Street' he left behind a musical legacy to be hugely proud of; one that has made Baker Street one of the most famous streets not just in London, but in the entire world. Not bad for a man whose music career started in his home town of Paisley, just outside Glasgow, with a folk-rock combo called The Humblebums, a band that bizarrely included the great stand-up comedian Billy Connolly on banjo.

While 'Baker Street' is an epic piece of lyrical writing, the song is arguably even better known for its iconic saxophone solo than its poetic content. There are two main reasons for this. Firstly, it is a sublime piece of playing, with a raunchy riff that introduces the song ahead of Gerry Rafferty's vocal before it then repeats as a chorus between the verses, soaring over the other instruments and binding the story together. The second reason is that the person frequently credited as being the saxophonist is none other than Bob Holness, that suave host of the old daytime kid's TV quiz, Blockbusters.

Even though many people genuinely believe that Bob Holness really did find the time to lay down this track between granting schoolkids' wishes to "have a P please, Bob," it is in fact an urban myth proudly claimed by the brilliant Stuart Maconie. While editor of the NME, Maconie ran a regular spoof 'Would You Believe It' column which contained outlandishly fictitious statements, such as Pet Shop Boy Neil Tennant being a fully qualified rugby league referee and that David Bowie invented Connect 4. None of these bits of fake news seem to have been believed in the slightest, but for some reason the claim about Bob Holness not only stuck, it became firmly embedded into folklore. This probably wasn't helped by the fact that Holness himself never appeared to publicly deny it, presumably as he was delighted to be associated with such musical greatness. And who can blame him?

In reality, the musician responsible for the sax solo was prolific session player Raphael Ravenscroft who sadly passed away in 2014, but his playing on that song is an especially fine way to be remembered. Astonishingly however, it was close to never having being heard at all as the saxophone parts that are now so integral to the song were originally imagined as guitar pieces. That was until Gerry Rafferty asked Ravenscroft to have a play around with the original guitar sections to see if he could come up with anything interesting. He did, and the rest is history.

It is almost impossible to imagine the song without those saxophone parts which are now legendary, but there is a recording of the original pre-sax track available on a remastered version of the 'City to City' album which was released in 2011, and is probably somewhere on YouTube as well. It's okay and certainly worth a listen out of interest, but it definitely benefited from that saxophone. Although that should not take away from the fact that the song also contains an excellent, but often overlooked, guitar solo from Hugh Burns which works superbly well with the sax to create the ambience of the city that makes the song so special.

But that sax solo is such a powerful piece of playing it's no surprise that I now have it stuck in my head and is all I can hear echoing around as I cross Marylebone Road after leaving the tube station. It's still a bright day, but despite all this cheeriness I'm afraid that my mood is about to change to darkness and gloom as it always does whenever I see the Victorian frontage of The Globe public house on this corner of Baker Street. For it was at this pub, back in the summer of 1985, that I suffered an incident that still haunts me to this day.

I was on one of my frequent trips to London and although I can't now recall the specific purpose of this visit, I remember that I felt in the mood for a quick pint before making my way down Baker Street. The Globe is well known to football fans who often stop there before catching the tube to Wembley, but on this particular afternoon it was full of office workers enjoying their lunch. Upon entering, I found myself a nice quiet spot at the corner of the bar, happy to stand and blend in while trying to avoid looking like a tourist. Although strictly speaking I was one, I never liked to be recognised as such because native Londoners always seemed to despise them, with their brightly coloured rucksacks, their Harrods carrier bags and their habit of stopping suddenly at the bottom of tube station escalators. I just wanted to look like a local and loiter incognito as I watched the world go by.

Out of interest, I browsed the tracks on the jukebox next to where I stood and was delighted to see that 'Baker

Rock & Stroll

Street' was listed. I couldn't believe my luck, that I had the chance to hear that song on the corner of the very street that inspired it - can you imagine how special that would be? So I inserted 50p for five plays and returned excitedly to my pint. After a few minutes the song began, with the gentle opening at first being drowned out by the chattering crowds. But then, as Raphael Ravenscroft roared into his introductory riff and it dawned on the hundred or so customers which song was playing, they immediately engulfed him with an uproar of groans, with gasps of "Not this again!", and moans of "Turn that off!" and "Bloody tourist!"

Having heard the jury's unanimous verdict in this particular court of public opinion, I was left feeling like a complete schmuck so quickly drank up and left the pub before they could critique the rest of my jukebox selection, or maybe even lynch me. I haven't dared to darken their door since.

While the dreadful memories of that experience will never be forgotten, I'm happy to say that my love of the song has not been harmed at all. Nevertheless, I still walk past the pub quickly just in case I get recognised, and don't slow down until I reach the junction with Paddington Street where I stop to look at the blue plaque on the wall of the premises where The Beatles opened their short-lived Apple Boutique in the late sixties.

Feeling in need of a sit down and some sustenance on my long walk, I pop into a pizza parlour on the corner of the street for a spot of lunch and am delighted to be shown to a table by the window. I always love a window seat so that I can meanwhile the time away watching the comings and goings of random strangers as they pass by

Rock & Stroll

and briefly, yet unwittingly, become dining companions. I hope they enjoyed the sight of me constantly pouring tiny amounts of beer from my large bottle of Peroni to refill the pissiest little beer glass I've ever seen.

Having finished my lunch I'm now back out on the road again, continuing along Baker Street which, at about one-and-a-half miles long, links the south-western corner of Regent's Park into Oxford Street. The fact that it's named after William Baker, the builder who planned and developed the street in the 18th century, reminds me how few of London's thoroughfares are named after the many influential women that have helped make the city the incredible place it is today. This is an observation that I probably wouldn't have been able to make if the point hadn't been so very well made by Sandi Toksvig in her excellent book 'Between the Stops', which I recently finished reading.

Baker Street was originally a high-class residential area well known for the grandeur of its properties but now, like many such streets, consists mostly of business and retail premises. As I pass one of those retailers, I have to smile at its name: The Sherlock Holmes Pharmacy. He manages to sneak in pretty much everywhere around here, but then it does seem appropriate that a character known for his frequent use of cocaine and various other narcotics should have a drug store named after him. I wonder if this is where he used to get his methadone?

A little further along I pass another retailer, one of a popular chain of health food stores, and can see an elderly man struggling to manage the door due to him carrying several large bags of shopping. I offer to get the door for him, but he just ignores my help and glares at me with a face that looks like he's just been licking dog piss off a stinging nettle. This only serves to confirm my long held theory that everyone inside health food shops, be they staff or customers, never looks particularly healthy or happy. Mind you, I can't say I'm surprised because back in the 1980s I followed a broadly plant-based diet myself, consisting mainly of hops and tobacco, and it did me no bloody good at all.

I'm now about halfway down Baker Street and I still have Raphael Ravenscroft's soul-stirring saxophone pitching around in my head so clearly it sounds as though it's echoing off the surrounding buildings. It may be well over forty years old but it sounds timeless and hasn't lost the ability to evoke an image of London that's as symbolic as a big red bus being driven over Tower Bridge. I think this must make it the most enjoyable earworm I've ever had, and as it accompanies me down the street I realise I'm even walking in time to it. That sure is the sign of a great song.

But while Gerry Rafferty's 'Baker Street' is undoubtedly one of the greatest songs ever written about London, Jethro Tull's 'Baker Street Muse' is surely the longest. Taken from their 1975 album 'Minstrel in the Gallery' and written by Ian Anderson, 'Baker Street Muse' is a sixteen-and-a-half minute suite consisting of five songs joined together, all written in the hard rock/folk style that Jethro Tull are famous for. It's arranged with a selection of lutes, flutes and strings that give an Elizabethan flavour, while electric guitars add a hard edge to the very contemporary themes of prostitution, homelessness and gutter journalism that feature in its lyrics.

Rock & Stroll

Collectively, it's a fascinating cluster of songs that make it feel like a night-time walk along Baker Street, or indeed many other city streets, as it casts a critical eye over the sights and sounds of such familiar things as Indian restaurants, newspaper vendors, buskers and filthy pavements. The lengthy saga then concludes with a spoken outro by Ian Anderson as he finds himself locked in the studio, trapped by his situation like the characters he's just been singing about.

It's a song that at first seems too long to listen to, but is packed so full of clever writing and musicianship it's surprising how quickly it reaches the end, and even then leaves you wanting more, which is a stroke of genius from the only band ever to be named after an 18th century agricultural engineer (unless you can think of any others).

Now nearing the end of Baker Street, I see a shop with a window display full of detective novels which, not surprisingly, features Sherlock Holmes prominently, and an accompanying sign that kindly informs me he actually used to live on Baker Street. No shit, Sherlock! But then again, having done some more elementary detective work it seems that Holmes' fictional address of number 221b was indeed a work of fiction because, when Conan Doyle wrote the novels, Baker Street was shorter than it is now and so the numbers didn't go as high as 221b. There can be no doubt though, that later crime fighting creations who were housed on Baker Street really did reside here, as 221b was certainly in existence when Basil the Great Mouse Detective moved in and when Danger Mouse set up home in the red pillar box outside it, while Sexton Blake also had lodgings nearby.

Rock & Stroll

As I'm walking on however, I must admit to feeling rather concerned as to just how safe the streets around here really are. Surely it's not such a crime hot-spot that we needed to have that many detectives living around here? And if so, I can't help thinking that if these great crime busting masterminds had concentrated more of their efforts on prevention rather than detection, then things might just have been a wee bit safer.

At the point where Baker Street becomes Portman Square, I turn right towards Upper Berkeley Street and then almost immediately left into Berkeley Mews, a drab backstreet that's little more than an alleyway. It's only about 200 yards long and hemmed in on both sides by typical bedsit mews properties, rear entrances to business premises, a pub and a car park. But the main attraction here today looks to be a squabble between two obese pigeons over the contents of a Burger King wrapper, and their antics immediately remind me of a strangely interesting little bit of trivia I recently learned that, on average, pigeons in London have 1.6 feet. This is supposedly due to such things as genetic disease, accidental injury or attacks by predators causing them to lose all, or part, of their feet, and mainly their toes. I'm not sure who carried out this research, or why, but it does bring an odd new connotation to the phrase "pigeon toed".

Since discovering this piece of information about our feathered friends, I have found myself taking more interest in pigeon's feet than is probably healthy, but from what I can tell the two examples I'm watching right now both seem to be fully endowed in the foot department. If they're not, it certainly isn't affecting their ability to brawl over the scraps of a flame grilled Whopper meal. So while

Rock & Stroll

its more prestigious relation Berkeley Square has singing nightingales, it seems that all Berkeley Mews has to offer is a pair of fat pigeons fighting over a ketchup sachet. And yet somehow it managed to inspire The Kinks' legendary frontman Ray Davies to write a song about it.

'Berkeley Mews' was released in 1970 as the B-side to their classic song 'Lola' and tells the story of a drunken romantic rendezvous in one of the houses on the street, which ended up in heartbreak. It begins with a honky-tonk pub piano style intro before rock & roll guitars kick in and drive the song towards an almost vaudevillian ending, which is a lot to pack into a two-and-a-half minute song that's frankly much more colourful than the street itself. As I stand here among these dreary surroundings, it seems a very unlikely setting for a song that was on the flip side of one of The Kinks' most celebrated recordings. But then Ray Davies was never averse to showing the gloomy side of London life in his songwriting, for although his clever lyrics are suffused with his deep love for the city he's also not afraid to shine a light into some of its darker corners. It's that eloquence and artistic mastery that allows his songs to capture the true essence of London, and the main reason that The Kinks are one of my favourite bands of all time.

It's possibly also one explanation as to why The Kinks never made it quite as big in America as many of the other great British bands of the 1960s, such as The Beatles, the Stones, The Who, Traffic, The Animals and Cream. Their music was quintessentially English and more London-centric than many of their peers, often focusing on our foibles and eccentricities while providing wry

Rock & Stroll

social commentary that may have been too satirical and unrelatable for listeners across the Atlantic to engage with.

It doesn't take long for me to walk the length of Berkeley Mews, but just before I reach the end I pass a delivery van that's parked up with its windows open and the radio on at pretty much full volume. Scoring high on decibels but low on street cred, it's blaring out Chesney Hawkes' 1991 mega smash 'The One and Only', that self-fulfilling prophesy of a song that was indeed the one and only hit he ever had.

Quickly returning to the main road, I fancy a stroll through the lovely looking Portman Square Garden that's just ahead of me. Okay, it's maybe not as impressive as New York's Madison Square Garden, but it still looks very pretty with its shrubs, lush green trees and beautifully manicured lawn. There's a sign by the entrance that informs me the park measures 1.5 hectares, is Grade 2 listed by English National Heritage and was built in 1780 on land owned by Henry William Portman (you were right again, Sandi). Unfortunately, there is also a sign telling me that the gate is locked and the park is only accessible to private keyholders. Well, I didn't want to walk through their snobby little park anyway.

Only slightly miffed I carry on walking the short distance up to the end of Portman Street, but I can already feel myself becoming increasingly anxious due to the fact that I'm also quickly approaching the fast and furious brouhaha of one of London's busiest and most frantic streets.

Chapter 5
Merchant of Menace

During my frequent jaunts to London as a young man in the 1980s and '90s, no trip could ever have been complete without at some stage calling in on Oxford Street. It was always the most vibrant and exciting place to visit, a fact borne out by the enormous amount of tourists from around the world who constantly crowded in for a piece of the action.

And of course, they still descend upon the capital's main shopping and commercial street in vast numbers, making it one of the busiest attractions in the city. Over 200 million people every year cram into its 1.2 mile fusion of flagship designer stores and numerous run-of-the-mill retail establishments, creating a West End shopping frenzy that Elvis Costello, in the song 'London's Brilliant Parade', referred to as an "occidental bazaar". Along with its multitude of adjoining streets, this is *the* place to be seen spending your money.

Originally part of a Roman road that linked Hampshire to Essex, Oxford Street was known as Tyburn Road throughout the middle ages when it also attracted many visitors, though for very different reasons than today. Back then people used to flood in to witness public

Rock & Stroll

hangings at Tyburn Gallows near the current site of Marble Arch. Up to 24 at a time they could manage - you can't beat a bit of good old family entertainment.

It later became a mainly residential street before gradually changing to commercial use by the late 19th and early 20th centuries when many of the country's first department stores started to open for business. The most famous of these was, and still is, Selfridges. Opened in 1909 by American Harry Gordon Selfridge, it was one of the largest and most upmarket stores in the world, boasting 50,000 square metres of retail space behind the grandest of facades, which still looks mightily impressive these many years later.

All of which played a considerable part in popularising Oxford Street to the extent that it continues to enjoy to this day, as it is high up on the list of pretty much every tourist's itinerary, whether visiting from inside the UK or abroad. For countless numbers of people believe that every outing to London has to include a visit to the place. This feeling was very accurately and succinctly expressed in the song 'Oxford Street' by Everything but the Girl on their 1988 album 'Idlewild', in which they conveyed the sentiment that London *means* Oxford Street. And there you have it: how Hull's Tracey Thorn and Ben Watt, the band's founder members, managed to encapsulate in a few simple words the seductive allure of Oxford Street. I think it's a shared emotion that's felt particularly strongly by many people like them, and me; the outsiders who missed the excitement of growing up and living in larger towns and cities, because Oxford Street was always seen as being the place where the big bad wide world began.

Rock & Stroll

At least, that's how it felt when I was younger. I have to confess that now I'm older it has lost nearly all of its appeal. Where it used to have a strong magnetic attraction, I'm afraid the poles have completely reversed to the point where it now quite frankly repels me and its entire length is just one vast, excruciatingly busy, pain in the arse episode of retail agony.

That's why if I need to travel along Oxford Street these days, I still prefer to walk but tend to do so along the side streets that run parallel to its length. It is so much better for avoiding the crowds as they are much quieter, less hectic and far more interesting both architecturally and historically. Every back street and junction appears to have a claim to fame or a blue plaque of some sort, and there is time to stop and admire the surroundings if you so wish.

But on this occasion, in the interests of research, I've decided to slog it out on the main drag of Oxford Street towards Tottenham Court Road, and I immediately remember why I now dislike this highway to hell and wonder how on earth I used to love it so much. I guess my spectacles must have been rose tinted in those days which is why I saw it as a street paved with gold, whereas now I just see pavements studded with gobbed-out chewing gum. And while I used to love all the hustle and bustle and hurly-burly of London in general, it's now those very same things that often challenge my devotion to certain parts of the city, and to Oxford Street in particular. It is practically impossible to walk its length without being pushed and jostled, or variously harangued, leafletted, charity mugged, market researched, fly pitched, Mormon wisdomed or Hare Krishna-ed. I very nearly managed it once, but then,

Rock & Stroll

just within yards of Tottenham Court Road tube station, I momentarily dropped my guard and got Big Issued.

The French philosopher and existentialist Jean-Paul Sartre once said that "Hell is other people". Well I don't know if he ever visited London, but if he did then I'm willing to bet he came up with that golden nugget of existential wisdom somewhere in the vicinity of Oxford Street.

But nonetheless I soldier on, suffering for my art, and as I pass a garish American-style candy store advertising "Marshmellows" - since when did that have an "e" in it? - I try to recall some of the memories I have of Oxford Street from earlier times, when it didn't give me the total ick. Things like the childhood excitement of browsing its tacky tourist souvenir shops (they're still thriving - anyone fancy a Prince William money box?); or seeing the long sweep of its twinkling Christmas lights for the first time; or the onion whiff of hot dog vending on a late autumn afternoon; or struggling to make out the message that man with the placard was always trying to convey, but without actually stopping to read it.

Ah yes, the man with the placard. He was a permanent fixture for years, walking up and down in his raincoat and peaked cap, usually in the vicinity of Oxford Circus, with his billboard held aloft proclaiming something about less protein meaning less lust, and hence more kindness. He also had a booklet available to purchase which spelled out his warnings of protein peril in more detail, but I never saw anyone give him anything other than a wide berth.

I researched him while writing this and discovered that his name was Stanley Green and that he'd devoted

Rock & Stroll

most of his later life to spreading his message. This might have seemed to most passers-by like the actions of an oddball but he treated it as a full time job, staying out in all weathers and keeping regular hours, including lunch breaks. Despite often being subjected to ridicule and abuse, it was a very personal crusade inspired by - well, I'm not actually sure what - but all credit to him for sticking at it. Because it was those dietary beliefs that gave him the passion and energy to continue his mission until he died in 1993 at the age of 78 following 25 years of promoting his ideals, so maybe there was something in it after all. I kind of wish I'd bought one of his booklets now.

In actual fact he appears to be more celebrated now than when he was campaigning, as Peter Watts, writing for The Londonist, dubbed Stanley Green "the most famous non-famous person in London", a description that's pretty accurate as everyone aged over forty that I've asked can remember him instantly. Renowned session bassist Martin Gordon even wrote a song about him for the solo album 'Include Me Out', which at least ensures that his protein dream will live on in music, if not on placard.

After a bit more Greco-Roman style jostling through the massed crowds, and with the formidable edifice of the Centre Point building looming ever larger at the end of the road, I arrive at Bond Street underground station. This featured on the picture sleeve of The Jam's 1978 single 'Down in the Tube Station at Midnight', the photograph showing Paul Weller, Bruce Foxton and Rick Buckler standing on one of the platforms while looking totally underwhelmed by the whole thing in that way that rock stars, especially the coolest ones, always seem to manage.

Rock & Stroll

The song begins with the familiar sounds of waiting passengers chattering on the platform as a train rushes in. This creates a sense of calm before the incessant high-hat cymbal, driving bass and slashing guitar appear and ramp up the tension before the urgent vocals of Paul Weller remind us how quickly normality can be ruined by the threat of late night inner city violence.

'Down In The Tube Station At Midnight' was the second single to be released from The Jam's seminal 'All Mod Cons' album and further demonstrated the influence that London had on their music. And like The Kinks, a band they greatly admired, The Jam weren't afraid to show the darker side of the city either, as shortly afterwards they released 'Strange Town', another song about London, in which they mention the unfriendliness of Oxford Street. And this is something I experience first hand as I continue on past Bond Street station.

In 'Strange Town' The Jam suggest that you should walk in straight lines, and I would have done well to remember that piece of advice before I veered off to the left in trying to avoid a cluster of slow moving tourists. In doing so, I managed to incur the considerable wrath of a tall, shaven headed man in his twenties who, had I looked before switching direction, I'd have noticed was not a man to mess with. His aggressive stride, straining neck muscles and taut frame shown off by a lack of clothing above the waist could have told me that. And just in case I needed any further clues, he had a look that said "Don't mess with me, arsehole!" etched permanently across his angry, contorted face like one of his many other tattoos.

But even so, I still didn't see him until it was too late and by then I'd already managed to trip him up. He stumbled, but somehow avoided falling completely, though not enough to save himself from feeling seriously offended. I immediately apologised, but clearly that wasn't good enough for him. He gave me a shove, fortunately not as violently as I think he could have managed (obviously I caught him on a good day), so I was able to quickly recover.

"I said I was sorry."

"You will be if you do that again!" he snarled, then walked menacingly close behind while making a couple of attempts to trip me up.

I thought about advising him that if he didn't like crowds then Oxford Street maybe wasn't the best place for him, but decided instead that discretion might just be the better part of valour. So I gradually moved towards the shop fronts and slowed down a little, pretending to window shop while he careered on ahead of me.

"Say that again and I'll punch your face in, twat!!" I retaliated, in a barely audible mumble as he disappeared into the distance on his bad tempered way. Now he really could have benefited from following Stanley Green's advice about eating less protein. The feckin' eejit.

This unhappy encounter has left me stirred and slightly shaken, with echoes of modern folk band Skinny Lister's excellent 2014 song 'Trouble on Oxford Street' reverberating around my head. But as luck would have it, I happen to be in the perfect place to stop a breather as I'm just outside number 363, the now empty shop that was always the focus of my journeys to Oxford Street and sometimes even the main purpose of my entire trip to London.

Rock & Stroll

For it was here that HMV opened their world famous record shop in July 1921. This then became their flagship store, except for a few years in the late '80s when their main store was on a larger site further along Oxford Street, before it became the flagship again in 2013. Sadly though, it completely ceased trading six years later.

That brought an end to nearly a century of music history, the pinnacle of which came in 1962 when The Beatles made their first recording here, cutting a demo using the store's production facilities. It was this which captured the attention of EMI records, who subsequently brought them to the attention of the world.

It was also here that I used to spend hours perusing the displays for any interesting new music, rarities, imports or special releases on vinyl, and later CD, that just weren't available in my local home town record shops. And if I couldn't find anything that appealed to me at HMV, there was always the Virgin Megastore at the Tottenham Court Road end of Oxford Street or Tower Records on Piccadilly Circus. All of these have now unfortunately closed down, victims of the enormous change in habits around the purchase and consumption of music.

Downloads and online retail have killed years of history, and while the computer age has certainly made access to music easier for many, the downside is that it's also ended much of the romance too. Scouring the internet isn't nearly as interesting as browsing the racks in a record shop and downloads completely lack the physical appeal and aesthetic presentation of a disc. Fortunately, vinyl has managed to make a modest return to popularity in recent years, partly for its novelty value, and there are still a

Rock & Stroll

number of avid collectors out there that enable some of the surviving independent record shops to carve out a niche. But it's heartbreakingly impossible to see how those mammoth music retailers could ever make a come back themselves.

  I miss those big old record shops so much, but I think it's the younger music fans of today that are really missing out. They might think they've got it made with their downloads and streaming, their Spotify and their Deezer, and they love to snigger at their elder's Amish-like grasp of technology. But nothing can replace the excitement we used to feel when we were given a record voucher for Christmas, knowing that it would give us the excuse to go music shopping. And in later life they will never experience that sentimental pleasure we children of the vinyl age get from rummaging through the sights and sounds of our old record collections; no-one remembers their first download, but no-one could ever forget their first record.

  My nostalgic urges are further intensified by the fact that the old HMV building still retains much of its original branded frontage, which whisks me back about forty years and gives me fleeting hope that it might actually have re-opened. Sadly though, the hefty steel plate welded into the doorway soon destroys that idea, but it's nice to see the old style 'His Master's Voice' lettering, along with the dog and gramophone logo, still standing as a shrine to its place in music history.

  I walk away in a wistful mood and, having finally had enough of the colourful collide-o-scope of Oxford Street, turn right into the relative calm of Bond Street. Actually, into New Bond Street, as although it continues

Rock & Stroll

almost seamlessly into the much shorter Old Bond Street they have never officially merged into one, a fact largely overlooked by pretty much everyone except a few die-hard locals. There was an attempt to unify the two streets in the 1920s but the residents, keen to protect their individuality, opposed the plans and the two have remained separate ever since, though the distinction between them is seldom made in everyday usage.

What's in a name anyway, especially when you can boast to be one of the most exclusive shopping streets in the world. Prada, Gucci, Chanel, Louis Vuitton, Armani, Bvlgari, Dolce & Gabbana, Cartier, Tiffany and Asprey all have shops here to attract the rich and famous, as well as the poor and curious, with their high end elegance. My wallet broke out in a sweat the moment I started following their Jimmy Choo footsteps along its pavement.

I did once purchase a unique perfume down here though, many years ago, a vintage bottle of Gingham eau de toilette that I bought from a street corner Del Boy fly pitcher, which did exactly what it said on the box - it smelled like a toilet.

Being on the edge of aristocratic Mayfair, Bond Street was a popular place for the upper class toffs of 18th century London to shop and socialise, and it quickly acquired a reputation for luxury and sophistication that remains to this day. It can claim some impressive former residents too, including the likes of William Pitt the elder, Lord Nelson, Jonathan Swift and Sir Joshua Reynolds. And intersecting New Bond Street near its northern end is Brook Street where, at numbers 23 and 25, lived Jimi Hendrix and George Frideric Handel respectively, both addresses now amalgamated as a museum to two hugely influential yet vastly different musicians.

Heading the opposite direction along Brook Street would bring you to Hanover Square which I remember visiting in the 1980s to feast at the Chicago Pizza Pie Factory. And if I recall correctly they had very cleverly given their toilets a musical theme, the gents being called the Elton John and the ladies the Olivia Newton-John. Geddit??

At the junction of New and Old Bond Street (Middle-Aged Bond Street?), two famous world leaders, Winston Churchill and Franklin D. Roosevelt, are honoured by life-sized bronze statues showing them seated on a wooden bench having a laugh and a chat. Sculpted by Lawrence Holofcener and unveiled in 1995 to commemorate fifty years since the end of World War II, 'Allies' is a charmingly relaxed portrayal of the two men who led their countries through the darkest days of the war. I have heard it said that the sculpture is a poor likeness of the two men, but I rather like it, and it's a very popular spot for tourists as they can sit between them and grab a selfie. In truth, it's about the only way most people can obtain a souvenir of Bond Street without breaking the bank.

Not surprisingly, the few songs to have been written about Bond Street reflect the high end exclusivity of the place. One such is 'Maid of Bond Street', a somewhat forgotten little ditty by David Bowie that tells of the unrequited desires of a fashion model who appears to have everything, except the man she loves. It's very early Bowie, from 1967, and while interesting to hear from an archival point of view, it has to be said that it's not one of his best.

Rock & Stroll

Some years later, in 2016, Andy Bell of Erasure recorded a song titled 'Bond Street Catalogues' about a girl who married a much older man solely for his money and the haute couture existence it would bring. The reality was much less glamorous however, as after a short time she became too busy being his carer to enjoy the luxury Mayfair lifestyle she was expecting. Oh well, serves her right I guess.

Although these two songs only achieved a modest place in the history of Bond Street, number 73 New Bond Street can make a much more significant claim to fame. For this was the site of the now defunct Levy Recording Studios where the 'Paul Simon Songbook', his first solo album, was cut in 1965. At the time, Simon was living in London and playing the club circuit, but the huge and unexpected success of this album caused him to return to the US and reunite with Art Garfunkel to become probably the greatest duo in popular music history.

As someone with little class and even less money, the bold as brass opulence of Bond Street is rather wasted on me so I leave its riches behind and head west along Piccadilly, certain to remain a Poundshop pauper for the rest of my days. From there I cross to the accurately described but unimaginatively titled Green Park and down towards The Mall, which is always a pleasant stroll. It is amazing how quickly a walk in the park can de-stress you from the tensions of the city and London is lucky to have so many of these green, open spaces.

I generally walk fast on the streets but in parks I tend to slow down a little to enjoy a bit of nature and some respite from the traffic noise. To be honest, I've found myself gradually slowing down anyway because my legs

Rock & Stroll

are tired and I'm feeling that I might have overdone it a tad with today's walk. I'm even beginning to doubt my long held belief that the best way to see London is on foot. But at least moving more slowly allows me to eavesdrop on the conversation of two young female students just ahead of me. To be honest, that wasn't particularly difficult at the volume they spoke while excitedly discussing their plans for a gap year. Now there's a subject guaranteed to raise the hackles of many of us oldies, especially those like me who had such an un-comprehensive education that a gap year was never an option. I left school on a Friday before starting work on the Monday - I only had a gap weekend.

It's not that I begrudge young people such as these who are lucky enough to be in a position where they can take some time out, but I do hope they appreciate how privileged they are, being able to spend a whole year poncing around New Zealand and Indonesia while brandishing their phones at the end of a selfie stick.

And talking of privilege, I emerge from Green Park straight into the formidable shadow of Buckingham Palace where the flag is raised, though I can never remember if that means the Queen is home or away. As usual there are large crowds of onlookers pressed against the fences or generally milling around and grabbing every photo opportunity they can get. One man I pass is even standing in the gutter of The Mall taking a picture of a mound of horse manure which was presumably dumped during this morning's changing of the guard. Well, I guess everyone needs a hobby.

Relating to the Palace, one of the most unusual songs featuring a London landmark that I've discovered is a lively reggae track called 'Buk-In-Hamm Palace'.

Rock & Stroll

Released in 1979 by former Wailer Peter Tosh, this number brings a real Rasta vibe to the most famous house in the city. That said, although Peter Tosh is reggae royalty, I doubt he would have been welcomed inside the Palace if he lit up and smoked the stuff he sang about in this song.

Having previously stood and looked at the exterior of Buckingham Palace more times than I care to remember, I don't bother hanging about on this occasion but instead turn right to head up the elegantly tree-lined Constitution Hill. So named not because of any reference to state rules or regulations but because King Charles II used to take his daily constitutional along here, it connects The Mall to Hyde Park Corner, running alongside the wall of Buckingham Palace Gardens as it goes. If truth be told the hill is barely even perceptible, but then I suppose Constitution Slope hasn't got quite the same ring to it.

During the 1840s Constitution Hill was infamous as the site of three assassination attempts on Queen Victoria, and so it seems rather fitting that it should also give its name to a protest song by Billy Bragg that appears on his compilation album 'Fight Songs'. While being quite Dylan-esque in its style, it has a very British message of political protest and reform and is sung without musical accompaniment to a slowed down version of an old 17th century tune named 'Lilliburlero.' This rousing march itself has historic links to revolution, yet despite that it's probably best known today as the call sign of the BBC World Service. Maybe those that see left-wing bias in the BBC's news coverage would say that's not a coincidence - now there's something for the tabloids to get their teeth into.

Rock & Stroll

Considering this as I walk along, it dawns on me that if the tabloids of the 1980s were to be believed then hard left Labour activist Billy Bragg may well have been the only Essex man not to have been seduced by Thatcherism when it swept across his county during that decade. Just as well, because no matter how hard I try, I simply can't picture Billy Bragg in Tory blue.

I bear left at the end of Constitution Hill to go down Grosvenor Place, still traipsing around the perimeter of the Queen's garden, and about halfway along I pass Chester Street. This predominantly residential thoroughfare progresses towards the heart of Belgravia and is therefore unsurprisingly prosperous. You would need to be seriously wealthy to live in these parts.

Brian Jones, guitarist and one of the founder members of the Rolling Stones, whose untimely young death was one of the first rock & roll tragedies, lived in a basement flat at number 13 Chester Street for a time during the mid-1960s. Having close links with fellow English R&B band The Pretty Things, Jones shared this grand Georgian house with them, which presumably led to the kind of lifestyle you would expect from sixties rock stars living in the heart of London. Such was the fun they had that in 1965 The Pretty Things even recorded a song entitled '13 Chester Street', a brash and zestful album track that added further to the infamy surrounding this address at the time.

Continuing a short way along Grosvenor Gardens and then turning left into Victoria Street, I find myself passing the Victoria Palace Theatre just as the audience is milling around outside having exited the matinee performance of 'Hamilton', the incredible hip-hop musical about

Rock & Stroll

America's founding fathers. A Sunday matinee is pretty rare in the West End but these lucky people have clearly enjoyed the show, and having seen 'Hamilton' myself on several occasions I can fully understand their excitement at having been present in the room where it happens.

Crossing the intersection towards Victoria station I pause to read the plaque at the base of Little Ben, the cast iron clock that stands on the traffic island. The inscription tells me that this charming nine-metre high replica of its big brother down the road was first erected in 1892, removed in 1964, and then returned in 1981, its refurbishment having been sponsored by Elf Aquitaine as a gesture of Franco-British friendship. In the spirit of that accord it also contains a rhyming couplet, credited to a certain J.W.R., that is a delightful apology to the French for the UK's policy of Daylight Saving:

"My hands you may retard or may advance
My heart beats true for England as for France."

Access from here towards Victoria Station is often a bit constricted due to the relentless flow of buses and taxis which, along with its narrow pavements, makes it very difficult for me to avoid being accosted by a slightly sinister looking man who thrusts a leaflet towards me as I try to walk past. I decline the offer by rounding him in an arc of just over an arm's length in radius but still catch sight of some of what's printed on the leaflet, and as I pass the general gist is further conveyed by some garbled conspiracy theory he spouts about the end being nigh. And if his railing against the world doesn't endear him to passers-by then I'm afraid his general appearance, clad in black and wearing a woolly hat and scarf that hides his features, doesn't help either. He certainly lacks the

Rock & Stroll

agreeable eccentricity that fellow forecaster of peril Stanley Green used to bring to his old patch on Oxford Street.

Entering Victoria and moving towards the tube station entrance, I chuckle to myself while recalling a discovery I made during my research for this book about the existence of a 1975 compilation album by Johnny Cash called 'Destination Victoria Station'. Thrilled at having found that a record by such a huge star had been dedicated to the station, it took a while for me to start questioning why a country music legend would be singing about a London mainline railway terminus. It didn't take very much more probing to learn that it had absolutely nothing at all to do with London but was actually made as a promotional record for a railroad themed chain of American steakhouse restaurants.

Fortunately, there haven't been too many other disappointments so far during this project and I'm pleased to say that, as I come to the end of this first day spent meandering around London's musical miscellany, the only problems I have are that I'm tired, my legs ache and I just want to sit down somewhere. So I'm very relieved that I don't have to wait long for the tube to arrive and I can begin my journey back home, and even more so that there are plenty of empty seats. I am worn out but have really enjoyed my day and made some great discoveries, so I'm happy and can't wait to head back down to The Big Smoke and do more of the same again tomorrow.

Rock & Stroll

Chapter 6

It's a Hard Rock Life

I'm sorry to admit that my second day of rocking around London Town starts off a fair bit later than I'd originally planned, mainly due to me being delayed this morning while carrying out some time-consuming and extensive research that has led to some fabulous new musical discoveries.

Okay, that's a lie. I was just exhausted from yesterday and so decided to sleep-in; you can call me a lightweight if you want to. On the plus side, at least I managed to miss this morning's rush hour which, despite its name, somehow always manages to spread itself across about three hours. But I'm here now and eager to get going again, having caught a Piccadilly Line train from St. Pancras down to Hyde Park Corner whereupon, on leaving the platform, I make a token effort to atone for my late start by running up the escalator (who's a lightweight now, huh?) and out into the street.

From there I head east towards Piccadilly, passing by the grand stone arches that provide a stately entrance into Hyde Park, the largest expanse of parkland within inner London. This brings back great memories of seeing

Rock & Stroll

one of my musical heroes, the legendary Paul Simon, perform there back in 2012. This was one of the regular summertime concerts that have been running in Hyde Park for over fifty years, the first one being performed by Pink Floyd in 1968. Since then there have been shows featuring such musical giants as the Rolling Stones, Queen, Tom Jones, Eric Clapton, The Beach Boys, Elton John, ELO, Bruce Springsteen, Madonna, and many, many more.

The Paul Simon concert that I saw, during which he and his excellent band performed the entire 'Graceland' album as well as many other classic songs, was one of several sponsored by the Hard Rock Cafe, which is rather fitting because that's where I'm off to right now.

Hard Rock Cafe is nowadays a global brand with a chain of music themed restaurants, bars and hotels, but the original cafe opened in 1971 at the Hyde Park end of Piccadilly and has been a popular eatery and meeting place for music fans ever since. During this time it has amassed an impressive array of rock memorabilia, some of which is exhibited in a museum called The Vault, situated just across the road from the cafe, and some is displayed on the walls of their restaurants, all of which, considering my writing project, makes this a perfect location for a spot of lunch.

As I said earlier, I am running rather late this morning because I'm tired after yesterday's exertions, but that's not the only reason. There is, in fact, another motive for my delayed start, as I have arranged to meet up with one of my oldest friends, a former school chum, for a chat and a meal at the Hard Rock.

Now I have to say that, for the most part, I absolutely hated my time at school. Whenever I hear

Rock & Stroll

anyone come out with that old saying about schooldays being the happiest days of their life, I can't help thinking they must have had a pretty shit life. I couldn't wait to leave, so when the time came I cut my ties with virtually everything and everyone connected with the place. But with one person I made an exception.

Jim Russell and I became pals at upper school back in the late 1970s, a time that coincided with the huge popularity of American TV drama serial 'Dallas'. Hence, his initials unsurprisingly led to him being saddled with the moniker "J.R." after the show's main character, J.R. Ewing. This always annoyed Jim, but much worse was to come a couple of years later when, while returning from a school trip, he threw up in the coach, an incident which naturally resulted in his nickname then evolving into "J.R.Spewing".

We always had a great deal in common (although, thankfully, not throwing up on buses) and many similar interests, as we both supported the same football team, enjoyed the same TV programmes and, generally speaking, we loved the same music too. Except, for some reason that I never quite understood, he liked Kraftwerk, while bumptious German synth-pop was certainly never up my strasse. Other than that, I think the only major disagreement we ever had about music was that I always fancied Jay Aston out of Bucks Fizz, whereas he preferred her bandmate Cheryl Baker.

Our later years at school saw us take quite different routes due to our O-level subject choices. I took a more academic approach and scraped unimpressive grades in Geography, German and Chemistry, whereas he chose Art and what was, back then, the new fangled option of

Rock & Stroll

Computer Studies, because he thought it would be a bit of a doss. From there our lives diverged even further as we entered the world of work, with me following a course of financial hardship through numerous unfulfilling jobs and him moving up the career ladder to build a reputation as a successful computer graphic designer. This brought him wealth, a big car, an expensive set of golf clubs and a house in the nice part of Hoxton, East London, while I barely have a pot to piss in. But despite his good fortune and prosperity I bear him no animosity at all, the bastard.

With that designer watch he always wears I would have expected his time keeping to be a little better, but he still manages to turn up at the Hard Rock Cafe nearly fifteen minutes late. Nonetheless, it's always good to see him, and today is no exception. He arrives slightly breathless, which at least suggests he's made a bit of effort to make up some of the time, and he's smartly, if rather brightly, dressed in his golfing gear ready for a game he has planned later that afternoon. He is a little taller than me and, if truth be told, has aged slightly better too, as he still has a full head of hair even though he chooses to keep it short. But at least he has the choice.

We exchange greetings and pleasantries prior to entering the Hard Rock, a venue I'd only visited twice before. The first occasion was back in the early '80s, then I didn't return until quite recently, this time with my daughter, Erin, an event made even more memorable when she nearly spat her food across the table in excitement at them showing a live Nirvana song on the big video screens that are dotted around the place. J.R. had only been here a couple more times than me, both of us having been put off by the fact there always seemed to be massive queues

Rock & Stroll

outside. Today though, we've wandered straight in with no delays.

Our waiter shows us to a table that looks out onto Old Park Lane and we immediately begin looking round at the music memorabilia displayed nearby. Mounted on the wall directly above our heads is Bob Dylan's Epiphone acoustic guitar and that's flanked by numerous other interesting exhibits, such as various items of clothing worn by The Beatles and Paul McCartney's old violin - I didn't even know he could play one. Behind where I'm sitting is an entire wall dedicated to Queen and Pink Floyd, and there are numerous photos, posters and mementoes of various other rock stars on show throughout the restaurant. This place is a rock fan's dream.

Sitting proudly by the bar are the two guitars that began the entire collection: a Fender Lead II donated by Eric Clapton and a Gibson Les Paul that arrived shortly after Clapton's guitar went on display, along with a note written by Pete Townshend of The Who that simply said "Mine's as good as his".

Having had a good look around, we settle down at our table and very soon our food arrives. We tuck in, having both ordered the same - Original Legendary Burger with fries and a bottle of Stella Artois - and the burger is excellent. No wonder the Hard Rock has been so popular all these years.

While chomping away, J.R. enquires about my book research and subsequent journeying around London. I try to look modestly embarrassed at being asked before then yapping on about it non-stop for a good fifteen minutes or so. He does well to look attentive throughout but has, not surprisingly, nearly finished his burger and is

Rock & Stroll

ready to order another beer while I've barely touched any of mine. I finally decide to tackle a few bigger mouthfuls which allows him to get a word in edgeways, galvanised into doing so by one of the music videos that are playing on the TV screens. While we've been chatting these have been showing artists such as Alanis Morissette, Wings, George Harrison, Lenny Kravitz, Madonna, AC/DC and The Verve, the latter of which is the subject of J.R.'s intervention.

"With all the research you've been doing you probably know this already, but The Verve shot those street walking scenes for the 'Bittersweet Symphony' video on Hoxton Street, really close to where I live."

I confess that I didn't know that, an oversight on my part, and thank him for the info. Not to be outdone however, I countered with the fact that The Beatles promo for 'Penny Lane' was filmed mainly on Angel Lane in Stratford, East London, to save them travelling all the way back to Liverpool for the shoot.

Stepping up to the challenge, he quickly came back with: "And they shot the opening sequence for the 'Hard Day's Night' movie at Marylebone Station."

I actually did know that, and so matched him with: "And did you know that a young Phil Collins was an extra in that film?"

J.R. then seriously upped the ante with a doozie about the incredible Joan Armatrading being a cousin of LibDem peer and kids' TV presenting legend Baroness Floella Benjamin.

Then, finally, I trumped him with the fact that Paul McCartney's younger brother, stage name Mike McGear, also had a number one record in the 1960s with 'Lily the

Rock & Stroll

Pink', as a member of The Scaffold. I then showboated with some extra details about the song also happening to feature Jack Bruce from Cream on bass and young unknowns Tim Rice and Elton John on backing vocals.

Aah, there's nothing much more satisfying than locking horns with another alpha male over a beer and some snippets of music trivia. A sure sign both of us are getting older.

Our conversation continued along those lines even after we'd finished our food and were quaffing our second beers, with more precious gems of not very useful music knowledge being unearthed and polished to a gleaming finish. Nuggets such as Spandau ballet being the flippant name given to the involuntary leg spasms exhibited by Nazi war criminals as they hung from the gallows at Spandau prison; the fact that The Monkees guitarist Mike Nesmith's mum invented Liquid Paper typing correction fluid; that environmental activist Greta Thunberg's mum once represented Sweden in the Eurovision Song Contest; that the first commercially available CD, released in Japan in 1982, was Billy Joel's '52nd Street'; and that Leo Fender, designer of the world famous Stratocaster and Telecaster guitars, couldn't actually play the guitar himself.

Having eventually moved on from talking about music trivia, we chat about various other things from our past before ending up, as we normally do, reminiscing about when he puked on the school bus - I know he never tires of hearing that story.

The time flies by, as it always does when me and J.R. get together, and before long it's time to argue over who will pay the bill. I insist on doing so as I think it

Rock & Stroll

actually is my turn, and besides, I feel guilty for having dominated most of the conversation.

While paying, we chat to the waiter who has been very friendly and pleasant throughout. I ask him if they get many famous people in the restaurant, to which he replies that they often do, but hadn't done so for a while due to the coronavirus pandemic restrictions stopping people coming out so much. I then enquired who was the last famous person that he'd served.

"Brian May came by here a few weeks ago," was his response. "He calls in quite a bit. He's a really nice guy."

That last bit didn't surprise me at all, as everybody I've ever heard talk about Queen's illustrious guitarist always says what a generous and charming person he is.

Having settled the bill, we head back out onto Piccadilly and before I know it, I'm bidding farewell to my old friend as he disappears off towards Hyde Park. It's been great to see J.R. again, but we must now head our separate ways as we both have lots of walking to do this afternoon, him around a golf course and me with loads more streets to visit. Luckily though, I won't be doing my walking in Rupert Bear trousers and an inexcusable salmon pink pullover.

Almost immediately after leaving the Hard Rock I see a blue plaque on the front of number 126 Piccadilly which, on closer inspection, informs me that this impressive building is where Francis Barraud created the famous image of Nipper the dog looking into a gramophone speaker. This artwork was known as His Master's Voice, the title of which was later abbreviated to give its name to the HMV record store chain, while the

Rock & Stroll

painting itself became the instantly recognisable emblem of the company.

From here, I begin to head further along Piccadilly which will take me to where I passed through yesterday while walking towards Green Park and Constitution Hill. So rather than just carry on ahead, I decide to ring the changes a little and divert off the main road for a change of scenery. To that end, I turn left to go up Down Street (or should that be down Down Street?), and from there I loop around Hertford Street and Shepherd Street before returning a little further along Piccadilly via White Horse Street.

Just on this short detour through the backstreets it's amazing what interesting and quirky things crop up. First of all, there's the disused Down Street underground station that is still easy to spot due to its deep red terracotta tiled frontage. Lack of passengers saw the station close down in 1932, but it got plenty of use during World War II as an underground bunker for Winston Churchill and the war cabinet.

Shortly after that I pass by the back end of the Hilton Hotel, then another blue plaque, this one marking the old headquarters of Radio Luxembourg, and then past the embassies of Panama and Thailand before reaching a couple of unusual restaurants. Firstly, there's a Polish/Mexican bistro, a combination that suggests some strangely unique menu choices (anyone fancy a gołąbki burrito?), and then a curry house whose windows are bedecked with photographs showing significant events that have occurred during its existence. The most notable of these commemorates the fact that it opened on the same day in 1963 that President Kennedy was assassinated,

Rock & Stroll

which brings interesting possibilities to that old saying that everyone can remember what they were doing when they heard JFK had been shot - dipping a naan bread into their lamb bhuna. Among the other mementoes are pictures of famous clientele which include a large photo of Michael Jackson, although I'm rather less impressed when, on closer inspection, I notice in the small print that it was in fact his brother, Tito, who popped in for a takeaway.

Following my diversion through the side streets I return to the ever popular Piccadilly, a major thoroughfare that is always synonymous with style and good taste. Its peculiar name derives from a successful local business run by Robert Baker, a tailor who specialised in the making and selling of piccadills. These were large, stiff collars made from lace that were fashionable during the 16th and 17th centuries and became so popular that Baker was able to make enough of a fortune to purchase much of the surrounding land and build himself a large house. His detractors mockingly called this Piccadilly Hall, but the soubriquet caught on and became the title bestowed upon the entire district.

After a short walk during which I pass The Ritz Hotel on my right, I find myself at the entrance to Burlington Arcade, one of the longest covered shopping galleries in Britain. Stretching nearly 200 metres up to Burlington Gardens, it contains a selection of exclusive boutiques, fine jewellers and luxury fragrance houses in a stylishly elegant setting that has barely changed since it opened in 1819.

Burlington Arcade is also famously known for its rules about whistling on the premises. Now, I don't know where you stand when it comes to whistling in public, but

Rock & Stroll

I've always found it to be a highly contentious issue that seriously divides opinion. Those that partake find it endlessly joyous, charmingly melodic and incredibly therapeutic. For building trade workers I think it might even be compulsory, it says so in the Magna Carta or somewhere, and they delight in sharing the dulcet tones of their tooting for all to hear. The rest of us however, find it really bloody annoying. But then I suppose there are far worse anti-social things you can do than create a criminally tuneless noise through pursed lips. Except, that is, on Burlington Arcade, where giving a little whistle could get you into a whole lot of trouble.

The reason for this is that while Burlington Arcade was hugely popular with the rich and powerful of 19th century London, it also attracted thieves and pickpockets in search of easy prey. This caused uniformed beadles to be employed to patrol the arcade, but when the various ne'er-do-wells observed a beadle approaching they would whistle out a warning to alert their partners in crime. This in turn resulted in whistling being forbidden, along with other lower class practices like singing, humming and running. That ban remains in place to this day and is still enforced by the Burlington Beadles, the oldest and smallest private police force in the world, who continue to patrol the arcade in their formal attire of braided Victorian frock coats and top hats - and very official they look too.

So, if by chance you should one day find yourself in Burlington Arcade and, despite my warning, you are caught whistling, how could you possibly avoid chastisement? Well, believe it or not, your best defence would be to try and convince the beadle that you are in fact Sir Paul McCartney, as he is one of only two people allowed to whistle in the arcade. This exemption apparently dates back to the 1980s when he was browsing the arcade and absent mindedly began to whistle. He was asked to stop, but once the beadle recognised the Beatle he allowed him to continue and granted him a lifetime exception to the rule.

The other person exempt from the ban is a young lad from the East End of London who had been experiencing some hard times at school. The beadles heard about this and promised that if he knuckled down and managed to do better with his education they would issue him with a permit to whistle. In 2011 he turned up at the arcade with a glowing school report and the beadles duly presented him with his permit.

I have to confess that I'm rather jealous of him, because whenever I walk down Burlington Arcade the very fact that I'm not allowed to whistle just makes me want to do it all the more. I'm sure it would echo really well too, especially with this classy tiled floor and its high ceiling.

Just as I'm wondering whether or not it's worth me trying to get away with it, I pass by one of the beadles as he's walking up from the entrance. Despite the authority suggested by his stately appearance he actually looks quite friendly and approachable, so I decide to chance my luck and enquire if the whistling ban is still in place, and if so how strictly do they enforce it.

Rising immediately to the challenge, he threw down a Victorian leather studded gauntlet, albeit metaphorically, and said "Well, why don't you give it a try and find out."

Rock & Stroll

Fortunately, this was said with a cheeky grin and a glint in his eye, and we went on to have a nice old natter for about ten minutes. His name was Mark and he had been at the arcade for about twenty years, during which time he'd progressed up to the position of head beadle and as such was the one who had issued the whistling exemption to the young boy.

During our chat he verified that everything I'd learned about the arcade from my research was true and even told me that Paul McCartney occasionally still pops in with friends, just to ask the beadles to confirm to them that he is indeed allowed the freedom to whistle. (This provides even further evidence to disprove that conspiracy theory about him dying in a car crash back in 1966). I also asked him if people do sometimes deliberately whistle as they walk through in order to get a reaction and he surprised me by saying that while most people obey the rule, the biggest offenders tend to be older men trying to impress their grandchildren on a day trip to London. But nevertheless, he assured me this was all done in jest.

From Mark's cheerful manner it's clear that he loves his job and seemed genuinely happy that I'd taken time to chat with him about the arcade and his position within it, and it was a pleasure to speak to him too. He is certainly a credit to the establishment and I have no doubt that the founder would have been very proud of him.

That founder was Lord George Cavendish, 1st Earl of Burlington, who commissioned the original plans to provide a covered arcade where the privileged and genteel could shop in comfort and safety away from London's filthy, crime ridden streets. It also conveniently served as a barrier to protect Cavendish's estate as he was sick of

Rock & Stroll

passers-by lobbing rubbish across onto his grounds, with oyster shells being a particular problem. Being very cheap and easy to eat, oysters were the working class fast food of the day - I believe back then McDonalds even did an Oyster McNugget - but then the shells would be discarded, in much the same way that pickled gherkins are today, and tossed onto the dear Earl's land without a care. So rather than faffing about and putting up a fence, he just built a luxury shopping arcade instead.

Being beyond the bounds of most people's budget, this elegant parade of sophistication provides a wonderfully fragrant setting in which to window shop, and the enduring classical air of the place was beautifully captured by Rick Wakeman and his son Adam who co-wrote and produced a track called 'Burlington Arcade' for their 1994 album 'Romance of the Victorian Age'. It's a jaunty instrumental piece that is well suited to the Regency style of the arcade's architecture, with predominant acoustic piano accompanied by electronic keyboards all played in a fast-paced, light rock style to a melody that would, rather ironically, be perfect to whistle along with. Oh go on, just this once!

Eager to avoid having my collar felt, I exit the arcade to continue east towards Regent Street. This takes me past Fortnum and Mason, Hatchards and the Royal Academy of Arts (I told you it was classy down here) and then past a sushi bar where a young couple at the window table are taking pictures of their lunch on their phones (okay, maybe not so classy). Whatever did we do for entertainment before we could share pictures of our meals with all our friends?

Rock & Stroll

A little further along Piccadilly, a young Asian man crossing the road trips as he steps up the kerb just in front of me and suffers a pratfall so comically perfect it would have served as a tribute act to all the slapstick greats, from Charlie Chaplin and Norman Wisdom to Mr Tumble and the Chuckle Brothers. Full credit to him though, as he manages to avoid total wipeout and recovers enough to move on swiftly as if nothing much had happened, giving just a quick nod in my direction. Caught between politely pretending not to have noticed the fall or giving a round of applause for the style of his recovery, I settle on a smile of solidarity and nod back.

Shortly after that I arrive at the busy road junction of Piccadilly Circus, the word "circus" in this context coming from the Latin word for circular as this used to be a traffic roundabout before being closed to vehicles on its south-eastern side. This is one of many London intersections named Circus that has brought disappointment to generations of small children who have arrived there expecting to witness a spectacular travelling show of Barnum proportions. For there is no big top, no plate spinning, no lion taming and no flying trapeze artists. But on today's showing there do seem to be a fair few contortionists, the odd clown, some piss artists, several performing jackasses and I believe they have the occasional knife thrower too.

Being right in the heart of the shopping and entertainment districts, Piccadilly Circus is one of the most popular meeting places in London. It is also very famous for its illuminated, though nowadays somewhat disappointing, advertising signs, and for the Shaftesbury Memorial Fountain around which the entire place seems to

Rock & Stroll

revolve. Commemorating the Victorian philanthropist and mental health campaigner Anthony Ashley-Cooper, the 7th Earl of Shaftesbury, the fountain is topped with a statue of the Greek god Anteros, dubbed the Angel of Christian Charity, although he is generally mistaken for his twin brother Eros, the god of love.

On the western side of the circus, the major American music retailer Tower Records used to occupy the premises that curve around the corner of Piccadilly into Regent Street. Opening in 1985, this was another favourite place of mine to come and enjoy the racks of vinyl and CDs along with their associated in-store displays, relaxed surroundings and knowledgeable staff. It was always a great place to visit until it finally shut down in 2009, another victim of the changing habits in modern-day music purchasing.

Musically, the Piccadilly neighbourhood features in several songs, most of which hail from the 1980s. For the album 'Go For It', Belfast band Stiff Little Fingers wrote 'Piccadilly Circus', a story about a violent and bloody assault on a man whilst out and about just enjoying the illuminations. This loud and aggressive song, with frantic guitars and punk attitude, is befitting of the subject matter and offers a much tougher sound of the streets than the Squeeze offering 'Piccadilly', which tells of a fairly unromantic first date consisting of a West End show and a curry. Released on the album 'East Side Story' this song is easily recognisable as a Squeeze composition, both musically and lyrically, and although these two numbers were both released in 1981 they provide very different insights into Piccadilly nightlife.

Rock & Stroll

Four years later The Style Council wrote 'Piccadilly Trail', a song of romantic disappointment and betrayal in the West End, and in 2006 The Feeling sang of similar experiences of lost love on the song 'Blue Piccadilly', taken from their 2006 debut album 'Twelve Stops and Home'. The following year, Everything But The Girl's Tracey Thorn also sang of heartbreak on her solo album 'Out Of The Woods' with the beautifully atmospheric 'By Piccadilly Station I Sat Down and Wept', a song that perfectly expresses the sorrow and loneliness that's often found in this big city. As so many songs written about Piccadilly appear to have romantic heartbreak as their theme, it seems fair to suppose that while this is a favourite rendezvous spot for couples, it's also a top spot for breaking-up too, so I can imagine there have been many people that have experienced those same feelings of sadness as they've sat down and shed tears by the station.

The oddest song that can claim 'Piccadilly Circus' as its title however, is surely the effort by Sweden's Pernilla Wahlgren whose 1985 entry into the national Melodifestivalen Song Contest only achieved 4th place yet still managed to became a public favourite. As the lyrics are in Swedish I have absolutely no idea what it's about, but it's worth a mention simply because the winning song in that year's competition was called 'Bra Vibrationer'. This number then went on to finish 3rd in the Eurovision Song Contest, despite (or maybe because of) its titillating title which apparently translates as good vibrations, although personally I'm not convinced about that.

Before leaving Piccadilly Circus I take a nostalgic look across to the south-eastern side and the corner of

Rock & Stroll

Haymarket, the place where, in 1977, I had my first ever Big Mac. Can you recall where you had yours? I'll never forget how it towered up from my little hand like a mighty Empire State Burger, and it will forever be remembered with a blue plaque on my heart and a grumble in my stomach. Somehow, they've never tasted so good since.

Heading up to the northern end of Regent Street towards the distinctive curve of its buildings and their stylish frontages, I see a little girl approaching with her family, happily playing a recorder which I guess is fresh out of Hamleys. To reference a well known musical phrase by a world famous pianist, I think she's playing all the right notes, but not necessarily in the right order, which generally seems to be the norm when it comes to playing the recorder. But at least she's not playing 'Frère Jacques'.

Although, as the name suggests, Regent Street was built during the Regency period, very little of that original architecture remains as it was largely rebuilt in the late 19th and early 20th centuries. During this time it became one of the world's first purpose built shopping centres, and as the curve straightens out its full splendour is revealed ahead of me. Every building was finished with an exterior of white-grey Portland stone and restricted to a maximum of five storeys to create uniformity along the entire street that is today a Grade 2 listed conservation area.

This attention to fine detail is probably why I never feel as rushed and ravaged on Regent Street as I do on many of London's other mainstream shopping streets. For although it's still a very busy retail thoroughfare, it's laid out like a spacious boulevard which gives it a more relaxed atmosphere and, at the risk of sounding snobby, a much classier feel. No doubt that's why The Kinks sent their dedicated follower of fashion shopping down here, even though the American pianist and guitarist Dan Bern paints a less complimentary picture in the song 'Regent Street', which features on his 2019 album of the same name. He sings of having a blurred brain, of dirt and grime and yet, despite all these grim thoughts, he still suggests keeping away from Regent Street as if it's the lowest ebb he could possibly reach. I dread to think what experiences he went through to make him feel that way about the place, but it's an excellent song and surprisingly uplifting considering the dark tone of its lyrics, with strident piano combining with brassy horns to make a boisterous blues-rock track. Roger Daltrey, a long time fan of Dan Bern, actually covered the song for a solo project some time before Bern even recorded his own version.

  I continue walking and, just off to the left, I pass Vigo Street which leads to Savile Row, world famous for its bespoke tailoring and also as the location of The Beatles' final live performance which took place on 30th January 1969. Held on the rooftop of number 3, back then the headquarters of Apple Records but now a branch of Abercrombie and Fitch, they played for forty minutes before the police arrived and told them to lower the volume, unceremoniously bringing the curtain down on the most influential band there has ever been.

  A little further along Regent Street and I turn left into Heddon Street, a smart, if fairly anonymous looking, U-shaped alleyway comprising several restaurants and bars with tables arranged on the pavement to give it the cafe culture vibe of a Parisian boulevard. Yet it's tucked away so neatly it would be very easy to walk past without realising its existence, let alone its place in music legend.

Rock & Stroll

For down here is the place where David Bowie posed as his alien alter-ego Ziggy Stardust for the cover of one of the most acclaimed albums of all time.

Released on 16th June 1972, 'The Rise and Fall of Ziggy Stardust and the Spiders from Mars' was Bowie's fifth studio album and an immediate critical and commercial success. While his previous works had brought many plaudits and generated a loyal following, his early career had also seen him suffer from several failed projects and some hard knocks. But these setbacks no doubt shaped the attitude and acumen that led to his success and longevity, and having re-invented himself at the start of the glam rock movement that he so vividly personified, it was this theatrical concept album that propelled him on a stratospheric rise to superstardom.

Preceded by the single 'Starman', the album tells the story of Ziggy Stardust, an alien rock star come to earth as a messenger to warn of the world's imminent end before following a path towards his own hedonistic self-destruction. As it was released during the time of the moon landings and an era when regular space travel seemed a viable future prospect, the album was an exciting concept; a piece of science fiction in music, where Bowie engaged the audience with the persona of an alien character possessing easily recognisable human traits in glam rock form. Musically, lyrically and stylistically, the album was light-years ahead of its time and put David Bowie at the forefront of both music and fashion innovation.

The album's front cover photo was shot right here, outside the entrance to number 23 Heddon Street, and showed Bowie dressed as Ziggy Stardust, posing with his guitar under a yellow sign that read 'K.West', the name of

Rock & Stroll

a fur dealer who occupied the premises at the time. The sign took on great significance as it was thought to have marked the beginning of the alien Ziggy's quest (K.West - good, huh?) to spread peace and love on earth. The original sign has long since disappeared, probably stolen by a fan unable to resist the lure of a priceless piece of memorabilia, and has been replaced by a plaque to mark the location.

While gazing up to read the plaque, I am approached out of the blue by a very smartly groomed American lady, about fifty-something I would guess, and looking not unlike Meryl Streep. She asks me to take a photo of her standing underneath it which, of course, I gladly do and we get chatting. Or at least she gets chatting, as is the case with many Americans she does like to talk. She is very pleasant though, and tells me she comes from Milwaukee. I pretend to know where that is, but in truth the only thing I know about it is that the sit-com 'Happy Days' was set there. Anyway, her husband apparently can't stand David Bowie so refused to come along, preferring to browse Oxford Street instead. Serves him right.

She, in contrast, is a huge Bowie fan and says she's wanted to visit Heddon Street for years, and that seeing the plaque was like visiting Mount Rushmore. Personally, I felt that was something of an over-statement, to claim that a 60-feet high rock sculpture of four US presidents that took fourteen years to carve was akin to a metal plate screwed into a wall on a Friday afternoon, but I admired her enthusiasm and kept quiet. On parting company with my new best friend we shook hands and she asked my name as we bade each other farewell, before telling me that hers was Ophelia Cox, but I think I misheard her.

Rock & Stroll

I move on up to the dead-end of Heddon Street, facing towards Regent Street, before stopping to look at the red telephone box that features on the back cover of the 'Ziggy Stardust' album, which shows Ziggy peering out at the world from behind the panes of glass. Even though this phone box has been unceremoniously tucked away in a dark little corner, it still attracts a huge amount of fans eager to replicate the scene in their own photos, despite the fact it's not the original one any longer. Indeed, even now as I'm looking on, it has a middle-aged couple trying to work out how best to capture the moment on their phones and another guy waiting to get in and have a look too. If Abbey Road has the most photographed zebra crossing in the world, then I'm sure Heddon Street must have the most snapped phone box.

Interestingly, these historic Ziggy Stardust album cover photos were taken by Brian Ward who had his photographic studio in Heddon Street itself. They were shot in black and white before being coloured in later by the renowned pop artist Terry Pastor, whose vivid handiwork created a theatrical superhero quality entirely in keeping with the theme of the record.

Before moving back onto Regent Street I turn for one last glance at this small street that has a big place in music history. It seems strange to think that when Ziggy Stardust fell here to earth this would have been just a poky little passageway of warehouses and workshops. Happily nowadays, it is a welcoming corridor of classy restaurants bustling with bohemian ambience that is certainly a fitting shrine to commemorate both Ziggy and the genius that created him.

Rock & Stroll

Chapter 7
Mourning Glory

It is very apparent when you cross over Regent Street that as well as being an architecturally attractive place to shop, it also plays a significant geographical and societal role within the capital. Serving as a dividing line between two distinctly different districts, it does a masterful job of separating upmarket Mayfair and its high-end clothiers to the west from the proletarian upstart dandies of Soho to the east.

Soho, bordered on its other edges by Oxford Street, Charing Cross Road and Leicester Square, is the busiest square mile of Central London and famous throughout the world for its fashionably bohemian nightlife and social scene. It is teeming with pubs, restaurants, coffee bars and theatres, and there is always a good chance of rubbing shoulders with celebrities that are often seen working or socialising in the locale.

Although there are several theories as to how Soho got its name, the most commonly held is that it comes from an ancient battle cry - "So Ho!"- believed to have been used by James Scott, Duke of Monmouth, during the 1685 battle of Sedgemoor in which he tried unsuccessfully to dethrone King James II of England. As the illegitimate

Rock & Stroll

son of Charles II, Scott had land bestowed upon him in the area which took on the name of his battle cry, and thence remained following his execution for his part in the failed coup.

Always a rousing and densely populated part of London, the 19th century saw Soho become a hive of poverty and deprivation with a notorious reputation for vice and immorality that continued well into 20th century. Its common image of thieves and prostitutes frequenting gambling dens, drinking clubs, strip joints and seedy nightclubs along a grimy maze of lanes and alleyways gave the district a menacing yet thrilling edge that visitors often found intoxicating. This sordid but seductive appeal was conveyed in two notable songs from the 1980s: 'A Rainy Night in Soho' by The Pogues and the title track of Phil Lynott's 'Solo in Soho' album, a reggae number carried along on an appropriate vibe of sleaziness.

Nowadays however, Soho is quite a salubrious place that attracts a much more cosmopolitan bistro, craft ale and Prosecco crowd, and while there are still a few fleapits and the odd dodgy looking backstreet I wouldn't want to risk walking down, it has pretty much thrown off its old identity.

Much of that transformation began during the 1960s as it evolved into the entertainment centre of London, with coffee bars, jazz clubs and music venues taking on an alluring new appeal as rock & roll became even more strongly established. This attracted a wider range of people to Soho that in turn gave it an increasingly bright and optimistic feel, making it a more fashionable and much safer place for locals and tourists to frequent, a

Rock & Stroll

trend which continues to this day. And right at the heart of that change in vogue was Carnaby Street.

Nowhere else can conjure up a picture of Britain during the Swinging Sixties quite like Carnaby Street. It was the coolest place with the hippest fashions, which placed it firmly at the cutting edge of all the developing music trends. Teddy boys, mods, glam rockers, punks and new romantics, they all flocked down here for their gear, making it the most vibrant shopping street in the world. So again it's no surprise that The Kinks' dedicated follower of fashion should have continued his voyage of discovery around these designer boutiques, marching on with the "Carnabetian Army" in tow, all intent on searching out the latest styles and modern trends along its pavement of mosaic psychedelia.

All of which made me slightly worried as I approached it, concerned that if it was still the same stylish place to be seen then I would struggle to fit in amongst the fashionistas. I am only too well aware that clad in my chain store whatnots to wear and sensible walking shoes I look like an advert for Primark.

But I really needn't have worried. These days it's full of people just like me, all in their fifties and sixties, searching for remnants from the past, both literally and figuratively. Their long forgotten treasures are now their best forgotten trousers, while wax jackets and orthopaedic slip-ons have replaced kaftans and winklepickers, and you're far more likely to see a comb-over than a quiff. There are still many clothing stores down here, but it's mostly mainstream retail chains that have muscled their way in, mixed with a few shops trading in tatty tourist clutter, rather than the individualistic fashion boutiques

Rock & Stroll

whose design flair put the place on the map by daring to be different.

Although it was always seen as being a bit more cheap and cheerful than its Chelsea rivals down the King's Road, it has to be said that today the whole street looks rather disappointing, not helped in any way by the underwhelming "Welcome to Carnaby Street" signs that arch across between the upper storeys of the buildings. Maybe I was expecting too much, but looking at it now it's hard to believe that this was once the epicentre of the fashion world as it sadly appears to be living on the memory of all its past glories.

This demise was even commented on as far back as 1977 in The Jam's 'Carnaby Street', in which Bruce Foxton sings in disillusionment at the passing of its prestige and hits the nail right on the head by saying it's not what it used to be. I'm glad it's not just me that thinks that.

I leave Carnaby Street from its southern end and wander along Beak Street which is named after Thomas Beake, one of Queen Anne's official messengers, who bought and then developed the surrounding land in the late 17th century. It's impossible to imagine a humble messenger having the financial wherewithal to buy a piece of land in this, or indeed any other part of Central London today. Approaching me, there is a happy young couple walking hand in hand, both clearly fans of musical theatre as the pair of them are proudly wearing T-shirts with motifs depicting West End shows. He's wearing 'Hamilton' while she's opted for 'Les Miserables', both shows which portray revolution through armed uprisings. I'm wondering if theirs is also a hard fought union forged through rebellion.

Rock & Stroll

From there I head deeper into Soho's tightly woven network of streets, turning left and then right into Broadwick Street, the birthplace of William Blake. Along this street there is also a preserved Victorian water pump which serves as a memorial to Dr John Snow and his discovery of the cause of a mass cholera outbreak that emanated from here in 1854. Broadwick Street crosses several other streets before reaching Berwick Street, another place with strong musical links, the most notable being that it provided the location for the cover photograph that adorned the groundbreaking Oasis album '(What's the Story) Morning Glory?', a recording which remains one of the UK's biggest selling albums of all time.

Released in 1995, the photo shows a blurry image of two guys about to brush shoulders while showing vague recognition of each other as they walk down the centre of the street. These two men are in fact the art director Brian Cannon and London DJ Sean Rowley, while to the left of the background is the record's producer Owen Morris who is seen shielding his face with the album's mastertape. This scene is easily identifiable as one of the strongest images of Britpop and another example of a piece of iconic album art being shot on the streets of London.

Berwick Street is also famous for having been home to many independent record stores, being particularly in vogue during the 1980s and into the '90s when the area was known as the 'Golden Mile of Vinyl'. Many wonderful music retailers thrived here, such as Sounds of the Universe, Sister Ray, Reckless Records and Vinyl Junkies. Again, most have been forced to follow the national trend which has seen three-quarters of Britain's independent record shops close down since the dawning of

Rock & Stroll

the new millennium. But some thankfully still manage to persevere, supported by loyal record collectors and nostalgia buffs, and down here on Berwick Street, resolutely staffed by a knowledgeable workforce, the few that survive even look to be flourishing and are well worth a rummage.

The rest of Berwick Street is like many others in modern day Soho, being full of general retailers, eateries and coffee shops, but is also the site of one of the oldest street markets still trading in the capital and where Marc Bolan apparently used to work on his family's fruit and veg stall during the 1960s.

Having crossed Berwick Street I continue along Broadwick Street to my next port of call, the historic Wardour Street, which connects Oxford Street to Leicester Square, cutting right through the heart of Soho as it goes. The site of a thoroughfare since Elizabethan times, it is one of the longest continuous streets in the area and is again largely made up of many busy restaurants and bars. During the 20th century this was an important location in the British film industry, being home to several big production corporations, and some smaller companies involved in movie making still exist here today.

It also has very strong links to the music scene, having played host to several famous live performance venues over the years. Up until 1967 The Flamingo Club was based here and was particularly famed for its jazz and R&B nights, with the Rolling Stones listed among its early acts, as well as being one of the first places to introduce Jamaican ska music to white audiences. Frequented by many established as well as up-and-coming musicians, it became known as The Temple in later years when it staged

Rock & Stroll

shows from the likes of Queen and Genesis, and later still hosted the Whisky-a-Go-Go club on its upper floors.

Number 203 Wardour Street housed The Vortex, a punk rock venue that was situated in the basement of Crackers Disco and which held gigs from bands such as The Slits, The Buzzcocks, Generation X, Sham 69 and Siouxsie and the Banshees. Notoriously violent, it is mentioned in the second verse of The Jam's 'A-Bomb in Wardour Street' which sets a tone of anguished despair as blood runs on the floor in a hate filled warning of apocalypse in the city, a reminder that violence and gang wars are not only a modern day phenomenon. The song is also another great example of the hostility The Jam regularly displayed towards London, for although they often wrote about the city, they rarely seemed to have a good word to say about it. But then, for a band whose array of songs encapsulated teen angst and the frustration of the masses, I suppose it's no surprise they should use their music to vent their anger and frustration at London life in a way that many people, myself included, can relate to. For as fantastic as London can be, it can all too often be downright bloody horrible.

Probably the most famous venue on Wardour Street would have been the Marquee Club which was situated at number 90, and during its time on that site, between 1964 to 1988, just about every major music artist performed there at some point in their careers. Whether just starting out or already established it was de rigueur to appear there, irrespective of genre, as the mix of acts that took to their stage was unbelievably eclectic: R&B, acid rock, prog rock, punk, new wave, synth pop - you name it, they played it. This undoubtedly made it one of the most

Rock & Stroll

important live venues in the history of rock and pop, and it's probably fair to say that without the Marquee many of the music legends we know so well today would have failed to break through and instead remained as modestly successful pub bands.

'90 Wardour Street' was also the title of a record released in 1985 by New York garage punk band Mod Fun. Heavily influenced by The Jam and the London music scene in general, they decided to name their debut album after the address of the Marquee Club, which is yet another sign of the influence it had around the world.

Sadly though, due to constant vibration caused by years of excessive high wattage output from its speakers, a 1987 commission found that the front of the building had moved slightly towards the pavement, so deemed its demolition necessary for safety reasons. Consequently, the Marquee closed its doors on Wardour Street for the final time on 18th July 1988, where an emotional performance from Joe Satriani brought their glorious past to a somewhat bizarre ending, with the club's steady pounding beat almost literally bringing the house down and so being responsible for its own demise.

Closely linked to the Marquee Club was The Ship pub which still very much exists on Wardour Street. Being just a few doors along from the music venue it was frequented by many artists who popped in for a drink following their sound checks at the Marquee, so famous faces were often to be spotted propping up the bar. One that wouldn't have been seen much though was The Who's drummer Keith Moon who was banned for letting off a smoke bomb in the gents toilet. The Ship was also mentioned in the song 'Born Slippy' by Underworld which

Rock & Stroll

became a hit after being featured in the film 'Trainspotting'. Written by Karl Hyde following a night's drinking in Soho that ended up at The Ship, it recalls, albeit in drunken sketchiness, his random, intoxicated thoughts and experiences on the journey back home to Romford.

Diagonally opposite Broadwick Street and just up from the site of the old Marquee Club is St Anne's Court which, from 1968 to 1981, was home to the world renowned Trident Studios. Countless major artists from that era recorded some of their most memorable work here, including Elton John, Queen, Frank Zappa, Joan Armatrading, Peter Gabriel, Lou Reed and David Bowie to name but a few, the latter also singing about the neighbourhood in his Soho soap opera 'The London Boys' in which he name-checks Wardour Street.

I emerge from St Anne's Court onto the upper end of Dean Street, another terrace of buildings steeped in history and which is particularly famous for its links to media, the arts and to London's jazz scene. It was also home to Gossip's (formerly Billy's) nightclub which is credited as having been instrumental in popularising the new romantic movement of the late 1970s and into the 1980s.

Going much further back in history, Dean Street is also where Admiral Lord Nelson finalised his battle plans the night before setting sail for the battle of Trafalgar, and in a more entente cordiale spirit the French House Pub served as the unofficial HQ of General Charles de Gaulle during his exile from France during World War II. Even further back than that, in 1764, a certain young Austrian boy named Wolfgang Amadeus Mozart played a piano

Rock & Stroll

recital at number 21 Dean Street while he was just eight-years-old.

Pressing on, I turn right by the Pizza Express Jazz Club and into Carlisle Street. There I pass one of those Beefeater souvenir dolls that seem to be so popular with very young tourists, although this one less so as it's laying broken and pathetically bedraggled in the gutter, presumably having drunk too much of it's own brand gin. Then I emerge into Soho Square which is lined along its sides with some very smart business premises. Many of these contain the offices of large media organisations which makes it clear to see why this stylish quadrangle has long been one of the most fashionable addresses in London.

Built during the 1670s it was originally called King's Square, and in its charming public gardens there is still a statue of Charles II, albeit well-weathered, sculpted by Danish artist Caius Gabriel Cibber. I stop for a while to admire it from a discreet distance, until a man wearing a geography teacher's brown corduroy jacket stands right in my eyeline. In the centre of the gardens there is also an unbelievably quaint mock Tudor oak beamed cottage that was erected in 1926 to conceal an electricity substation. Why can't all substations be made to look that picturesque?

Featuring in music, sixties band The Tremeloes wrote 'Negotiations in Soho Square' about two young lovers meeting by chance in this small green park before beginning a romantic affair, while in 1993 there were, coincidentally, two songs released with the title 'Soho Square'. Newcastle folk rockers Lindisfarne wrote about lonely out-of-towners having their heads turned by

Rock & Stroll

London's flamboyant women whilst visiting the square, but without doubt, and I'm sure they won't mind me saying this, their effort was easily outshone by the wonderfully moving composition written and performed by Kirsty MacColl.

Released on the album 'Titanic Days', it tells a sad story of growing old while waiting for the return of a lost love to celebrate her birthday at an empty bench in Soho Square. Written and sung in Kirsty's distinctively street-wise yet vulnerable style, it's made even more emotive by the way her life ended so tragically at the ridiculously young age of 41.

While holidaying in Mexico in December 2000, she was diving in a designated safe area of the Cozumel National Marine Park when a speedboat entered the restricted area and sped towards her party. Having managed to push her two sons to safety, she was sadly then unable to make her own way clear before the boat struck, killing her instantly.

Kirsty MacColl was born in Croydon, the daughter of renowned folk musician Ewan MacColl, and being a South London girl it's no surprise that many of her songs were acutely observational of a very British way of life. They were full of poignant yet witty lyrics that were reminiscent of The Kinks, and indeed one of her biggest solo hits was a cover version of their classic song, 'Days'. In addition to that she had a wealth of other hit records that appealed to lovers of many musical styles spanning new wave, folk, country, pop and rock. Being married to acclaimed producer Steve Lillywhite, she also sang backing vocals on several albums produced by him for artists as diverse as Robert Plant, The Smiths, Simple

Rock & Stroll

Minds and Talking Heads. She was a true crossover artist who proved that genuine talent is comfortable in any genre.

But her most famous hit came, of course, when she duetted with Shane MacGowan on The Pogues' 'Fairytale of New York', that perennial festive favourite that even people who hate Christmas songs generally agree is a classic. And I, for one, never tire of hearing it. So perfect is her rendition of that song, it's amazing to think the female vocal part was originally intended to be recorded by The Pogues' bass player Cait O'Riordan. She, however, left the band before the track had been finalised, leading producer Steve Lillywhite to once again ask Kirsty to step in and bring her vocal prowess to the final recording. She went on to make it her own and it has been a national favourite ever since, becoming the most played Christmas song of the 21st century. What a wonderful legacy.

In 2001, a memorial bench in tribute to Kirsty was unveiled near the southern entrance gate of Soho Square and bears an inscription taken from the song of that name. This song was always a fan's favourite and every year they hold a ceremony here to gather together and sing in celebration of her life. This takes place around the time of her birthday (October 10th) and so fits perfectly with the lyrics and the spirit of the song.

Although the bench isn't particularly easy to find, especially when it's in use, it really is worth taking the time to locate it and quietly reflect on the tragedy of her death, as well as the glory of her life. As I do so, I choke back a tear while I recall the lyrics of 'Soho Square' and enjoy this beautiful spot that somehow manages to be amazingly tranquil considering it's just a stone's throw away from the mayhem of Oxford Street. It's a simple but immensely touching memorial to the life of Kirsty MacColl, a woman that I honestly believe is one of the greatest, yet also one of the most underrated, recording artists of all time.

And I'm sure she would have loved it here.

Rock & Stroll

Chapter 8

Caffeine Hit

Gonzalez, that long-forgotten UK combo best known for their worldwide smash hit 'Haven't Stopped Dancing Yet', recorded a jazz instrumental in 1974 called 'Funky Frith Street'. In doing so, they immortalised in smoking saxophone and tight guitar grooves the street that runs down from Soho Square to Shaftesbury Avenue. But just what is it about Frith Street that makes it so funky?

For a start, it featured heavily in the 1986 Julien Temple movie 'Absolute Beginners' which was predominantly set in and around Frith Street. Or at least, in a stylish, tightly packed version of it constructed at Shepperton Studios. Although, on reflection, that's maybe not the best example because the film bombed terribly, despite its star-studded cast and excellently designed sets.

So what else is funky? Well, as with most of Soho, Frith Street is a busy and vibrant thoroughfare lined with properties that nowadays primarily accommodate business premises, but were once spacious townhouses that can claim John Constable and the Mozart family, including young Wolfie, as past residents. It also shares a cosmopolitan ambience with its parallel neighbour Greek Street, and as that once provided lodgings to 18th century

Rock & Stroll

Italian lover boy Giacomo Casanova there can be no doubt he would have frequented Frith Street in search of female company. The world famous Ronnie Scott's Jazz Club has resided here since 1959 and that is certainly funky, listing among its numerous musical highlights the final live performance by Jimi Hendrix, on 16th September 1970. And just opposite are the premises where, in 1926, television pioneer John Logie Baird first demonstrated the transmission of images from his workshop in the attic. And occupying that space below the attic of number 22 Frith Street today is Bar Italia, one of the most famous and, to my mind, the funkiest coffee shop in the whole of London.

Opened in 1949 by the Polledri family and still owned by them to this day, Bar Italia was a central hub of the large Italian community that had settled around this part of Soho in the post-war years, putting it at the forefront of the coffee bar craze that erupted during the 1950s. As countless more followed, these became favourite haunts not just for Italians, but for everyone else to congregate. And as the rock & roll scene also exploded about that same time, the links between coffee bars and popular music were emphatically forged, with Bar Italia being particularly popular with mods.

By the 1960s there were around 500 of these new coffee bars in Greater London alone, predominantly attracting a younger clientele that was eager to discuss and discover new music. They made proper coffee using the new Gaggia espresso machines, sold good, simple food and, as they were almost all independent businesses, each had an individual character of its own. All this in stark contrast to today's boom in identically bland coffee shops

Rock & Stroll

run by corporate bean counters, hitting the market with their allegedly dubious tax arrangements and unFairtrade working practices. (I think I should say allegedly again, just to be on the safe side).

Bar Italia itself is fascinating. It immediately evokes the ambience of a classic Italian cafe, with tables and chairs laid out on the pavement below an eye-catching wall clock with a neon surround, all pervaded by that unmistakably rich and bitter-sweet smokiness of freshly ground coffee. It's original interior was state of the art 1950s and, despite being partly updated, remains much the same today, with red and white Formica, a stylish Gaggia coffee machine that's over 50-years-old and a Roman-style mosaic tiled floor. It is adorned with sugar shakers, flags and newspaper cuttings with photos of mainly Italian sporting successes and showbiz relevance. Behind the counter is a large poster of former regular customer and boxing legend Rocky Marciano along with a pair of his boxing gloves, and on the back wall is a massive TV screen that appears to show mostly sports channels, but is also a nice nod in the direction of the upstairs attic where Logie Baird could only have dreamed of such a thing.

Being so snazzy it's no surprise that it often attracts celebrities as well as tourists and also inspired Pulp to include a song about it on their 1995 Mercury Music Prize winning album 'Different Class'. The lyrics are conveyed affectionately by Jarvis Cocker as he sings of sugaring up his coffee on the way home from an evening's clubbing, saying it's the only place to go for a late night/early morning caffeine fix. Natalie Imbruglia also mentions drinking coffee at dawn in Frith Street on her song 'Glorious', so again making reference to Bar Italia's 24-

Rock & Stroll

hour opening times that make it a regular stop for night-time revellers who fancy delaying their journey home with a lattè. Furthermore, it has been the subject of many articles and photo shoots over the years, was featured heavily in 'Absolute Beginners' and has even been suggested as the subject for a stage musical.

But above all, it is a damn fine coffee shop with an incredibly authentic feel to it. I often visit whenever I'm in London, and a coffee with biscotti always feels like a treat. Today is no exception and it's great to sit inside and enjoy the usual sights, sounds and smells that transport me all the way from London to a cafe in the backstreets of 1960s Turin. So much so that while peering out to watch the world pass by the doorway, I fully expect to see first red, then white and blue Mini Coopers racing past, being chased towards the mountains by the polizia in their green Alfa Romeos. And as I hold the coffee cup to my lips, I swear I can hear Michael Caine telling me "You're only supposed to blow the bloody froth off".

I am suddenly shaken from my daydream by a waitress who appears alongside me to take away my plate and in doing so causes me to dribble the last slurp of my Americano. Having woken up and spilled the coffee, I wipe the Italian blob from my chin and head off to continue my journey, happy to have once again enjoyed a visit to Bar Italia.

Revived by my caffeine boost I walk briskly down to Old Compton Street, itself being another place written into the history of London's espresso revolution of the mid-20th century and its links to the rise in popularity of rock & roll. As with the rest of Soho, many trendy coffee bars sprung up along here too, and as most were opened

Rock & Stroll

by immigrants this was reflected in the diverse characteristics of their establishments which added to the appeal for a young and trendy crowd in search of new music, whether live or on the jukebox. Cafes such as Heaven and Hell, Act One Scene One and the Algerian Coffee Stores were all hugely popular as youth culture really took hold. But it was the 2i's Coffee Bar that really shook things up, so much so that it's still revered to this day for the influence it had on rock & roll and for the hit makers that performed here.

Opened in 1956 by two brothers with the surname Irani (hence its name), the 2i's was soon sold off as the brothers moved on to open a nightclub nearby. It was bought from them by a couple of Australian wrestlers who kept the original name and began to stage live music down in the basement. This attracted skiffle groups to play which naturally then led to rock & roll, a transition that put the club at the forefront of this new genre as the craze swept the nation and attracted young people from miles around, all eager to either see or be the next big thing.

Due to the fast growing reputation of the music venue, leading industry movers and shakers regularly came along to check out the new talent that played there and sign any that showed promise. Hence, the 2i's was responsible for launching the careers of many exciting and well-known performers, such as Thomas Hicks, Terry Nelhams, Brian Rankin, Reg Smith, Clive Powell and Harry Webb (more commonly known as Tommy Steele, Adam Faith, Hank Marvin, Marty Wilde, Georgie Fame and Cliff Richard respectively). Joe Brown was also discovered there, but wisely declined the pseudonym of Elmer Twitch that was suggested by his manager, the

Rock & Stroll

famous impresario Larry Parnes. Had he taken that name, it's possible he may never have been the major influence he was at the dawn of British rock & roll or had such an incredibly long career either, because Joe Brown is such a cool, everyman name that it simply didn't need changing. And certainly not to Elmer Twitch, which sounds more like an affliction than a stage name.

Even though it closed down as long ago as 1970, the 2i's is still widely regarded as being the birthplace of British rock & roll and the popular music industry that followed, and a plaque to that effect is mounted on the wall of its premises at 59 Old Compton Street to this day. As I read the plaque, I contemplate how much coffee bars have changed since then, and that while there has been a modern day surge in the quantity of coffee shops (you'd be hard pushed to find a single street in Central London that doesn't contain at least one), we seem to have sacrificed quality and individuality. This certainly seems to be the case as far as the nationwide chains go. For although, as a nation, we now consume coffee in volumes the rest of the world can only marvel at, I can't see this predominantly conglomerate driven industry giving us anything we could be as historically proud of as the 2i's.

Nowadays it seems to be more about the superficial rather than the substance, for while the Filofax and mobile phone used to be in vogue, the steaming paper cup is now the accessory to be seen with. And coffee isn't simply coffee any longer, but more of a Wonka-esque confection that takes ages to construct. I've had to become used to queuing for ages while the people in front order their yabba-dabba-chinos, agonising over which species of milk to choose and then what size, shape and hue they want,

Rock & Stroll

from flat and white to tall and skinny. Then they cram in calories with various swirls, shots and sprinkles before topping off with the obligatory cocoa-dusted emblem, as we've become so obsessed with our own self-image that even our hot drinks need to display a tattoo.

I just want a coffee please, not a concoction, and I certainly don't want the torture of waiting behind some guy who's texting his girlfriend to see if she wants mango syrup in her turmeric latté while the barista faffs around making him a smoothie.

Beverage Luddites of the world unite, and I'll see you back at Bar Italia.

As well as being famed for its coffee bars, this part of Soho is also prominent in the film and TV industry, with many production companies having offices around here. This is touched upon by the Scottish born singer-songwriter Al Stewart in his 1969 song 'Old Compton Street Blues', a moving and intricately woven tale of a failed actress-come-model who frequented these streets. In her search for fame she found only exploitation and minor roles in TV adverts, leaving her with just a few faded magazine photos to show for her dreams.

From Old Compton Street I wander down to Shaftesbury Avenue, heart of London's Theatreland, where my own personal experience of the local media and entertainment industry is fleeting, but I'm pleased to say comes with happier memories. For along the approximately 300 metre stretch of pavement between Greek Street and Wardour Street, I have, over the years, randomly encountered ex-footballer Lee Chapman, TV chef James Martin, actors Tom Conti and Simon Callow (twice), and Hollywood legend Morgan Freeman - that's

Rock & Stroll

right, I said Morgan Freeman - and I believe he still talks about it.

Then I turn left onto the southern end of Wardour Street as it heads down towards Leicester Square, passing through the always colourful and captivating heart of Chinatown as it goes. First settled in the 1920s, London's Chinatown has grown in size and status to become the largest commercial Chinese enclave in Europe and is awash with supermarkets, herbal medicines, lanterns, waving cats and more restaurants than you can shake a chopstick at.

It's somewhere round here that Warren Zevon, during his 1978 novelty hit 'Werewolves of London', bumped into a werewolf with a menu in its hand that was looking for Lee Ho Fook's restaurant. In order to find it, he would have had to turn left into Gerrard Street, on the corner of which I now stop to watch an excellent busker playing electric guitar and singing the Oasis track 'Wonderwall'. And I have to say, at the probability of enraging a Gallagher brother, he does it with somewhat greater gusto than Liam sang his own rather lacklustre song that was dedicated to this part of the city. But in his video to 'Chinatown', Liam Gallagher is shown walking through these very streets so it would have been a marvellously appropriate track for the busker to have segued into, but instead he does 'Song 2' by Blur, which at least keeps the Britpop rivalry alive.

In 1980, Thin Lizzy also released an album called 'Chinatown' with a title track full of guitar riffs that are unmistakably theirs. And as lead singer Phil Lynott did on his aforementioned 'Solo in Soho' album, released earlier that same year, it again highlights the seedier side of Soho

Rock & Stroll

which is much more hidden away these days, but I'm sure still exists if you really want to go looking for it.

I turn off Wardour Street shortly before I get to Orange Street which, whenever I'm nearby, always makes Madness' debut single 'The Prince' come bounding into my head. Disappointingly though, this Orange Street runs tamely between Haymarket and Charing Cross Road, so rather lacks the musical kudos of the one in Kingston, Jamaica, that Madness sang about as the heartbeat of reggae, rocksteady and ska, as well as being the birthplace of music legends Dennis Brown and Prince Buster.

Despite being about as far from uptown Jamaica as you can get, both geographically and culturally, the spirit of that ska beat helps me shuffle along to Leicester Square where I pass by M&M's World, a massive four storeys of prime retail space all dedicated to a fairly mediocre kid's sweetie. Whatever next I wonder - Malteser Land? Parma Violet Planet? I always preferred Treets anyway. As I'm walking past, a group of girls in their late teens are leaving the shop and one is having a meltdown because she's just broken one of her fingernail extensions - quick someone, call an ambulance.

I walk on from the drama and venture further into Leicester Square, so called as it was built on a piece of land acquired by the Earl of Leicester who originally envisaged it as an aristocratic residential district. At least, that was the idea when it was first planned in 1670, but those classy intentions changed in the late 18th century as some of the initial buildings were demolished and replaced by centres of entertainment. Artists then quickly followed, it all got very bohemian and everything started heading downmarket. Not so much fun for the nobility any longer,

Rock & Stroll

but loads more fun for everyone else, because while Soho is generally accepted as being the 24-hour party capital of Central London, it's Leicester Square that does much of the heavy lifting in that respect.

Being the entertainment hub of the West End, its pedestrianisation in the 1980s gave it a much needed boost after the 1979 Winter of Discontent, during which dustbin collectors were among the many groups of striking workers that brought the country to its knees. This resulted in Leicester Square effectively becoming a rubbish dump as uncollected refuse piled up on the streets, earning it the clever, albeit rather demeaning, nickname of Fester Square.

Walking through here now it's very hard to picture that scene, as this is one of the busiest districts of London and is always thronging with vibrant energy no matter what time of the day or night. Being particularly appealing to young adults, it attracts millions of visitors every year in search of entertainment among the many restaurants, bars, theatres, street performers and casinos it boasts, as well as several flagship cinemas that often stage star-studded film premieres. But with competition now so tough between cinema chains and against online movie streaming, it has been told to me by an industry insider that the films they screen nowadays are pretty much loss-leaders as they cut admission prices to lure customers into their core financial business of selling popcorn by the bucketload. So the next time you visit Leicester Square, just bear in mind you are in fact at the very centre of the UK's popcorn industry.

As the square opens out, I pause to watch one of several street entertainers on show today, an Elvis

Rock & Stroll

impersonator who sounds uncannily like Tommy Cooper - "dog, hound/ hound, dog" - but I then swiftly walk on as the man in front of me spits onto the pavement, a habit that has become depressingly common in this country. It seems that being rude and uncouth is now the preferred way of sticking two fingers up to the rest of society and offenders sneeringly wear their vulgarity like a badge of honour. Strange to think that not so many years ago we proudly claimed to be world leaders in good manners and etiquette, and how alarming it is that our standards have plummeted as rapidly as an empty Red Bull can being hurled from the window of a speeding car.

All of which is unfortunately rather rancid, but at least that conveniently allows me to mention the American punk revival band of that name who released a song called 'Leicester Square' on their 1998 album 'Life Won't Wait'. And while I personally am glad to leave punk rock a good long spitting distance back where it belongs in the 1970s, Rancid is still a brilliant name for a punk band.

And just to emphasise the excitingly diverse nature of London's influence on music with a completely different style of song, Jethro Tull released a number called 'Jeffrey Goes to Leicester Square' which first saw the light of day back in 1969. So this little hive of humanity bustling around a clump of trees on the edge of Soho has not only inspired a screaming, thrashing, angst-ridden punk song of pent up alienation, but also a flute and electro-balalaika driven folk rock song of mild annoyance. The only thing square about this place is the name.

Now nearing the end of Leicester Square and just outside Burger King there's a wonderfully charismatic Afro-Caribbean street magician entertaining a crowd of

Rock & Stroll

onlookers, and I wonder what on earth magicians would have done had packs of playing cards never been invented.

A short wander further along and I'm in Cranbourn Street, looking over at the opposite pavement towards the Charing Cross Road entrance of Leicester Square tube station which is cryptically referred to by The Feeling in their previously mentioned album 'Twelve Stops and Home'. This title refers to the number of stations on the Piccadilly Line from Leicester Square to Bounds Green, the area of North London where lead singer Dan Gillespie Sells grew up. Today, the station entrance is looking even busier than usual, a sure sign that rush hour is now well under way and people are desperate to get home, hampered in doing so by increasing numbers of visitors starting to descend upon the area for an evening's entertainment. I fear those twelve stops to home will be very uncomfortable and frustrating this evening.

On the corner of Charing Cross Road as you leave Cranbourn Street is the legendary London Hippodrome, which opened in 1900 and was planned by renowned theatre architect Frank Matcham. With a grand exterior that's as strikingly impressive as is its history, it was originally designed as a venue for circus and variety acts and incorporated a sunken arena that was capable of being flooded with 100,000 gallons of water to allow elephants, polar bears and various other aquatic species to perform. This made it a perfect location for the English premiere of Tchaikovsky's 'Swan Lake' in 1910 and it then continued as an innovational performance hall, hosting what is believed to be the UK's first official jazz concert in 1919, appearances by Harry Houdini and, many years later, the stage debut of a 12-year-old Julie Andrews.

Rock & Stroll

During the 1960s it found world fame as The Talk of the Town nightclub and concert venue which staged productions featuring the biggest names in showbiz from both sides of the Atlantic. These included Judy Garland, Frank Sinatra, Sammy Davis Jr., Shirley Bassey, Tony Bennett, Tom Jones, The Carpenters, The Jackson 5 and Stevie Wonder to name but a few. In the early 1980s it reverted to its original name of The London Hippodrome but as a nightclub and restaurant, before becoming the casino and entertainment complex it is today.

Shortly before changing back to its initial title, The Talk of the Town also lent its name to a single by The Pretenders, and while the lyrics of that song didn't mention the venue itself, the record cover had the imposing red and white neon signage from above the main entrance emblazoned across its sleeve.

A confessional song of unrequited love, 'Talk of the Town' was written by Chrissie Hynde and sung in her usual warm and shimmering style - as sultry as a summer's day - with the late James Honeyman-Scott adding a light breeze with his distinctive jangly guitar playing. The sound is unmistakably that of The Pretenders and this track still sounds great today, serving as a reminder of just what a fantastic band they were and that their enduring influence and artistry is, I feel, often overlooked.

Emerging in the late 1970s and crossing over into the 1980s, The Pretenders were inevitably dubbed as a new wave band but they skilfully transcended that tag, challenging the wisdom of pigeonholing music to genre according to the era in which it finds popularity. Why consign a band as good as this to a brief, prohibitive corner in time, especially when they've left such a strong musical legacy?

Taking most of the plaudits was Chrissie Hynde on guitar and vocals, fronting the band with a seriously cool and feisty attitude at a time when there weren't very many women fronting bands at all, and certainly not as commandingly as she did.

From Charing Cross Road I continue into Long Acre, finally saying goodbye to Piccadilly, farewell to Leicester Square and so long to Soho, that simmering stockpot of so many mixed ingredients and seasonings that brings umpteen different flavours to the palate. It's hearty and zesty, full bodied and fruity, it's got bite and can be sweet or sour, and even a little bit tart, yet it still leaves an intense espresso kick on the aftertaste.

Despite Soho's long held reputation for petty lawlessness and organised crime, as well as its strong links to the sex industry and associated deviant activities, there have also been plenty of colourful characters, creative geniuses and shrewd visionaries that have helped make it the funky, cosmopolitan heart of the city that it is today. As far as London is concerned, Soho is still the talk of the town.

Rock & Stroll

Chapter 9
Squaring the Circle

Roddy Frame, that wistfully charismatic Scottish troubadour and frontman of the now defunct Aztec Camera, claimed in a radio interview to have named his fourth solo album 'Seven Dials' after spending much of his time in London around that particular area. And when you visit this aesthetically charming locality just north of Covent Garden, it's easy to see why it would have appealed so much to him.

This historic road junction where seven streets converge, forming an imperfect circle around a tall white column to create a 17th century version of a traffic roundabout, should be utter chaos. But in actual fact it seems to work pretty well and is more attractive and noticeably calmer than many of the other nearby streets. This despite it still being a major draw for shoppers and tourists who are drawn to the independent boutiques, restaurants and arty-crafty lifestyle stores that line the narrow cobbled streets and courtyards which emanate from the junction into the prosperous district that bears its name.

Roddy Frame's album, released in 2014, also includes a reference to Seven Dials in the lyrics of the

Rock & Stroll

third track, the reflective and silky-smooth 'Into the Sun', where he infers that a lost soul can never find its way out of here. That's a sentiment with which I have to agree, because I usually find this labyrinth of streets quite disorientating myself.

This is due to the way it was laid out by local MP Thomas Neale during the 1690s, as he planned the development to be a series of triangles with their apexes all meeting at a central point, meaning that if you struggle with trigonometry, you're basically screwed. But there was method in his madness, as he had calculated that by using the available area in this way they could erect houses with longer frontages, and as rentals were charged per foot of frontage rather than square foot of interior, he would be quids in. The original plan was for six roads to meet at a central intersection around a large, multi-faceted sundial, featuring one dial for each road. But a seventh road was added during construction, no doubt as another means of generating rental income, which rather spoiled the initial concept of the sundial design, as it had already been constructed with six faces. After a bit of quick thinking however, they announced that the column upon which the dials were mounted would itself act as the gnomon to cast its shadow across the circular junction, which would in turn become the seventh dial.

The idea behind the development was to build an upmarket quarter that would capitalise on its close proximity to the desirable Covent Garden Piazza, but over time the area became a deprived slum leading the poet John Keats to call it the place "where misery clings to misery, and want and disease lie down side-by-side, and groan together." Not exactly a great Tripadvisor review,

Rock & Stroll

but fortunately the 20th century saw a long-term regeneration project that resulted in it becoming the fashionable locale it was always intended to be.

The tall Doric pillar that today stands in the middle of the junction with the sundials sitting on top is not, in fact, the original, but an accurate replica of the one that was designed by stonemason Edward Pierce. His was pulled down in 1773, allegedly by a local mob in search of buried gold, although that story may be apocryphal. It's still an impressive centrepiece though, and another great example of a piece of history that's easy to miss unless you stray from the main roads and explore off the beaten track.

Doing just that inspired Madness on their critically acclaimed 2009 album 'The Liberty of Norton Folgate', which features several songs that reference various lesser known parts of London. Included on the 3-disc special edition boxed set is a song called 'Seven Dials' on which Suggs sings fondly of strolling the narrow alleys around here as the sun's rays catch the faces of the dials. And as I leave Seven Dials, I do what I'm sure countless people have done before and instinctively check my watch against the shadows being cast, and sure enough we agree on the time. Had they differed, I think I would have trusted the dials over my own timepiece.

I wander away from this relative calm via Earlham Street and head north up Charing Cross Road. Once there, I am quickly reminded of the harsh realities of city life as I pass a couple arguing loudly on the pavement, acting out their domestic strife in public like it's the climax of an EastEnders story line, but without those dramatic "doof, doof" drum beats. Aah, EastEnders - London's very own soap opera, where family is everything, except when

Rock & Stroll

they're cheating on or murdering each other. Bless 'em, those cheeky little Cockney sparrows. Then, further along, I see the now sadly familiar sight of two seemingly empty duvets laid out in a large shop doorway and get the shock of my life when one of them suddenly moves to reveal that it's currently being lived in.

A short distance after that I pass Foyles, one time Guinness Book of Records holder for the title of world's largest bookshop in terms of shelf length, racking up an astonishing total of 30 miles. Then I turn off to the right and into Denmark Street which was a fairly unremarkable residential thoroughfare when originally built in the 1600s, but gained much kudos shortly after completion for being named in honour of Prince George of Denmark, consort to Queen Anne. Yet much later still it became decidedly more prestigious as the hub of the British music industry, a position it held during most of the 20th century.

Music publishers initially began to populate this short street due to its close proximity to concert halls and theatres, so they could buy new material from songwriters before selling them on to performers. Other related trades soon followed and over time it became filled with promoters, recording studios, musical instrument stores and music journals including Melody Maker and New Musical Express, both of which were produced from here. This led to it becoming a one-stop shop for commercial music and subsequently being dubbed Britain's Tin Pan Alley, a nickname derived from New York's West 28th Street, the historic home of their music publishing industry.

Looking at a quiet and slightly shabby Denmark Street today it's difficult to believe it could have played

Rock & Stroll

such a massive part in the evolution of popular music throughout the 1950s and '60s, but its influence cannot be underestimated. Many emerging and established songwriters plied their trade around here, working with publishers and artists keen to find new material and promoters looking to discover the next big star. All this creative activity generated a potent mix that drew in crowds of aspiring musicians, each of them wanting a piece of the action.

That sense of raw excitement, when new songwriters were being signed up daily by publishers, was captured by The Kinks in their song from 1970 that bears the name of the street, before then offsetting that optimism by hinting at the grim reality of exploitation and failure many of those hopeful artists experienced at the hands of their fickle pay-masters. It's a typical Ray Davies song set to a delightfully chirpy music hall tune with perceptive lyrics that paint an amusing picture of what Denmark Street must often have been like at the time. And they would have known better than most, because the management company Denmark Productions, based at number 25, handled their affairs during the 1960s.

One ambitious musician that was drawn here was a young office boy named Reg Dwight who took a job at Mills Music, a renowned publishers, that was based at number 20 Denmark Street. This put him in the right place to get a foot on the ladder and make contacts in the industry that he loved and that he would, of course, later come to fabulously enrich as Elton John.

In his 1975 song 'Bitter Fingers', Elton sings about Denmark Street and echoes much of the sentiment expressed by The Kinks, with Bernie Taupin's lyrics

Rock & Stroll

providing an insight into how demanding and thankless a task it could be trying to please the agents as you hawked your music around the different publishers. Like The Kinks, John and Taupin were very familiar with Denmark Street, for as well as having been employed down here as an office boy, Elton recorded cover versions of hit songs for budget label Embassy who were also based on the street. They were responsible for those cut price compilation albums that Woolworths used to sell. You must surely remember them - they're the ones we got for Christmas when our parents wouldn't buy us the real thing, and despite our disappointment we still tried to look grateful because at least it was better than getting poked in the eye with a shitty stick...but only just. In Elton's defence though, he and Bernie Taupin are rumoured to have written 'Your Song', their first hit record, on Denmark Street, so I guess he can be forgiven.

Among many other notable artists to have written or recorded material that originated from the street are Donovan, Cat Stevens (who lived in nearby Shaftesbury Avenue), John Paul Jones, Jimmy Page, Bob Marley, Jimi Hendrix, The Who and the Rolling Stones, whose debut album was produced down here in 1964. Mention must also be made of the great Lionel Bart, that prolific songwriter and composer of 'Oliver!', who began his career here and later became known as "the King of Denmark Street."

The movers and shakers didn't always get it right though, as the great Paul Simon, to name just one, had all his early compositions turned down by several of the street's publishers for being "too commercial." Some of those rejected songs went on to become timeless classics.

Rock & Stroll

The street was also famous during the 1960s for La Gioconda, a posh sounding but rather shabby looking cafe situated at number 9 that was a popular meeting place for many of the musical types that worked down here, as well as for eager hopefuls trying to make their way in the business. David Bowie was a die-hard regular who met his first backing band there and a young Marc Bolan was a frequent visitor too, as were the Rolling Stones. They would probably have rubbed shoulders with the likes of Eric Clapton, Jeff Beck and the Small Faces, while latterly The Clash and the Sex Pistols also patronized the coffee bar before it was finally decaffeinated in 1992.

By then a lot of the old music business crowd had moved out after the industry underwent massive changes during the 1960s and '70s. The old crooners and music hall acts were a dying breed who were being replaced by bands and solo singers, many of whom were writing their own material and singing of personal experiences that their younger fans could relate to. As a result there was a declining need for performers to buy songs off-the-peg, so the music publishers and agents began to move out, taking many of the associated businesses with them.

Denmark Street today still retains some links to the music industry however, but mainly the retail side, being home to a thriving abundance of shops selling musical instruments and sheet music. And at least it remains a maverick at heart, managing to avoid becoming a tourist retail trap despite its close proximity to Oxford Street, and while it may no longer be so cutting edge, it's still a gathering place for serious musicians. Indeed, in just the short time it took for me to walk the length of the street, I saw a man in his late twenties struggling along with what I

Rock & Stroll

assume was a double bass, all zipped-up safely inside the biggest gig-bag I've ever seen. Then, just after he'd passed me, I saw a much older, white haired man in a kilt trying to conceal a set of bagpipes under his arm while colourfully bedecked with a matching tartan scarf and deerstalker hat. I often wondered what happened to the Bay City Rollers.

Over recent years much of this neighbourhood has been subject to redevelopment as part of the massive Crossrail infrastructure project that has seen the demolition of several buildings in the surrounding area and threatened many more, with Denmark Street not being left totally unscathed.

The building and expansion of this major transport hub, at the junction of Charing Cross Road and Oxford Street, has already forced the closure in 2015 of the 12 Bar Club, a small music venue of only about 100 seats but with a history that belied its size. Opening in 1994 on the site of an old stables at 26 Denmark Street, it went on to stage performances from big names such as Adele and K.T. Tunstall early in their careers, as well as from more established artists like Jeff Buckley, Keane, Roddy Frame and Bert Jansch, who recorded a live album there. And as the commitment to redevelop the area continues around nearby St Giles Circus, there is still much uncertainty about the future of Denmark Street, with its past seeming to count for very little.

Back out onto Charing Cross Road, I head up towards Tottenham Court Road tube station which has been completely rebuilt as part of the Crossrail project. The new station exterior certainly looks far smarter and more modern than the dull and dilapidated old building,

Rock & Stroll

but it again comes at a cost to the London music scene as the Astoria, which stood near this junction, was closed in 2009 and subsequently demolished to make way for the newly developed station. Much bigger than the 12 Bar Club, with a capacity of around 2000, the Astoria hosted gigs from some of music's biggest names over its 25 years as a leading performance venue, with many shows having been recorded and released as live albums and DVDs.

Standing in the shadow cast by the colossal Centre Point tower, it occurs to me that the entire area around this junction seems to have been under construction of some sort or other for as long as I can remember. Since Centre Point was completed in 1966 as one of London's first skyscrapers, it's been a never-ending building site around here and I honestly can't recall a time when I haven't seen it populated with hard hats, cranes, scaffolding and cement lorries. Today is no exception. Perhaps the massively delayed Crossrail development will at last be the culmination of a project that appears to have seen virtually every building in the area undergo major refurbishment, demolition or reconstruction. It certainly gives credence to the old saying that "London will be a great city when it's finished."

Outside the tube station a busker is playing 'Sultans of Swing' with some wicked licks on his electric guitar, and while I'm watching a passer-by asks me the way to Oxford Circus. I point them the right way along Oxford Street, which will take them past the massive Primark that now stands on the site of another one of my regular haunts from the past - the Virgin Megastore. Of all the major record shops in London this one always had the most exciting vibe to it, I guess because it's founder, a pre-

Rock & Stroll

knighthood Richard Branson, was still cool and seen as a bit of a hipster. Or maybe I just get that sense of excitement because it always brings back personal recollections of an all too brief encounter.

Let me take you back to the summer of 1984 when I was a denim-clad nineteen-year-old, keenly browsing the record racks on one of my first solo trips to London. Now I haven't mentioned this yet, but I am a massive Billy Joel fan and have been for years. I love the variety and complexity of his music and have seen him live in concert numerous times. Had he ever written a song about London then it would be all over this book, but he gets a mention here solely because, on this memorable occasion, I had found a newly released 12-inch single (remember those?) of 'Tell Her About It' and was at the cash desk waiting to pay for it.

Having reached the front of the queue, the assistant called me forward. She was a very attractive girl about the same age as me but with a completely different style, quite punky, with short, spiky blonde hair, jet-black eyeliner and a nose stud. As she took the record from me she glanced down at the cover and declared: "Ooh, I love him."

I was more than a little surprised, but then Billy Joel does appeal to a wide audience, I guess even to some punks, so she was obviously a closet fan who hadn't yet "come out." Let's face it, he may be the third biggest selling solo artist of all time (by album sales), but even I would have to confess it's never been particularly cool to publicly admit liking him.

Or maybe she fancied me? Yes, that must be it. After all, I was a bit of a good looking dude back in those days, even if I do say so myself.

Rock & Stroll

"He's great, isn't he! He's been a big influence on me," she continued. "And I love his hair."

Oh my God, my hair looks just like his on this record cover. She really does fancy me.

"He's a brilliant musician," I spluttered, trying to look all James Dean while quickly thinking of a killer chat-up line. "Er...what's your favourite song?"

She slipped the record into a carrier bag and, as she did so, her face dropped down through her studded leather trousers and straight into her knee length Doc Martens.

"Oh...I thought that said Billy Idol."

And that was the end of our beautiful friendship.

*   *   *

I continue north along Tottenham Court Road, depressingly passing by a couple more homeless people huddled in shop doorways, until after about a quarter-mile I turn left into Goodge Street, the quirkily named thoroughfare that leads into the historically avant-garde district of Fitzrovia and which featured as a song on the 1965 Donovan album 'Fairytale'.

'Sunny Goodge Street' is a gently meditative jazz/folk composition that's been covered by the likes of Marianne Faithfull, Judy Collins and Paul McCartney, although they were obviously luckier than me to find a 'sunny' Goodge Street, because now the evening is drawing in the skies are frowning and it's starting to drizzle. This is causing my mood to dampen a little, but that kind of fits in with the song as it starts off quite mournfully before picking up a tad as Donovan sings about smoking hash and getting the munchies. He then walks on through mystical neon lit streets that settle into a

Rock & Stroll

psychedelic stillness as he mellows to the music of jazz great Charlie Mingus. As well as being vividly colourful this is also quite an historic song, having been one of the first to be played on national radio that made explicit references to drug use and its effects.

This impressionistic vision led to Goodge Street gaining a reputation as a place to acquire and consume illegal substances (Ah, so *that's* why it was always sunny) and its pubs and cafes became hippy hang-outs, all of which further enhanced the area's beatnik credentials.

Exiting Goodge Street to the right, I progress up the north end of Charlotte Street which was named in honour of Queen Charlotte, the wife of King George III. This street kindly lends its name to a song by Lloyd Cole and the Commotions that featured on their 1984 debut album 'Rattlesnake', which implies a furtive romantic liaison in one of the many basement flats along here. I'd wager it's likely to be one of many that's occurred along this very artsy, culturally hip roadway that among the townhouses also contains numerous offices, restaurants and pubs, the most famous of which is undoubtedly the Fitzroy Tavern. Commemorating the Fitzroy family, the Dukes of Grafton, who owned much of the land on which Fitzrovia was developed, the tavern has been frequented over the years by many of the writers, poets, artists and intellectuals that have settled in this district, including Dylan Thomas, George Orwell, Virginia Woolf, George Bernard Shaw, Ezra Pound, John Constable and Walter Sickert.

Just before Charlotte Street becomes Fitzroy Street I detour off, via Howland Street, to Cleveland Mews so I can pass directly under the BT Tower, Fitzrovia's most

Rock & Stroll

prominent landmark. Standing 190 metres high and completely dominating the local skyline, it's visible from just about everywhere around here, which makes even more amazing the fact that on completion, due to being critical to the national communications network, its location was protected by the Official Secrets Act and so did not appear on any maps. Looking up at it now from ground level makes me feel so queasy and vertiginous, it's very difficult to see how anyone could pretend that this huge cylindrical edifice doesn't exist.

Previously known as the GPO Tower, the Post Office Tower and Telecom Tower, it was constructed to transmit telecommunication signals using microwaves rather than underground cables, all of which must have sounded like a piece of science fiction when it was built in the 1960s. And even despite its age, it still looks quite futuristic to this day, albeit with a hint of Heath Robinson eccentricity thrown in. Among the features it originally contained were viewing galleries and a revolving restaurant, all officially opened to the public on 16th May 1966 by Tony Benn and Billy Butlin (now there's a double act that never caught on) and was, at the time, the tallest building in the UK.

The BT Tower also features on the cover photo of a 2013 album by established jazz/funk musicians Bill Sharpe, keyboardist and founder member of '80s band Shakatak, and Jah Wobble, bass player with Public Image Ltd. (The origin of the name Jah Wobble apparently comes from a drunken pronunciation of his real name, John Wardle). On the cover, the tower looms large over the surrounding buildings under the ornately framed album title: 'Kingdom of Fitzrovia'. This is also the name of track

Rock & Stroll

number 3, a smooth and mellow instrumental piece featuring prominent keyboards and brass underpinned by the kind of fluid, funky bassline you'd expect from such a renowned bassist and perfect for chilling out on a lazy day in this genteel quarter of Central London.

Back out onto the main road I continue up to Fitzroy Square, the assumed capital of the Kingdom of Fitzrovia, and very grand it is too. Conceived by Charles Fitzroy, 1st Baron Southampton, and designed during the 1790s by Scottish brothers Robert, William and James Adam, it consists predominantly of Portland stone fronted four-storey townhouses with basements, all built in a classical Georgian style. Historically and architecturally magnificent, it surrounds a sizeable and beautifully maintained private gardens which puts me very much in mind of the closing scene from the movie 'Oliver!', when the title character finally finds a home and is ushered in by his great-uncle.

Much of Fitzroy Square was destroyed during the blitz of 1940 but subsequently rebuilt to resemble the vast splendour of the original, before being extensively pedestrianised during the 1970s. This development wasn't universally popular as it removed some of its vibrancy, but the reduction in traffic noise must surely have improved it as a place to live. It is certainly still elegantly, and expensively, very upmarket, and has been home to many notable people throughout the years, borne out by the fact that almost every other house appears to have a blue plaque or an ambassadorial flag attached to its facade.

But all this grandeur makes the sight of another homeless person on one of the benches around the perimeter all the more striking, as he looks so out of place

Rock & Stroll

snuggled into a tatty sleeping bag in such affluent surroundings. As I pass by, I offer him a couple of pounds which he accepts with charming politeness.

Like most people, I find it increasingly difficult to comprehend the amount of London residents that are either homeless or scraping an existence in vulnerable housing and employment, and hard to reconcile this underclass against the immense wealth and privilege that the rest of the world knows our capital city by. You can't escape the poverty and deprivation that has undoubtedly grown over the last decade or so, but seeing it juxtaposed in such stark contrast to these opulent surroundings makes it even less palatable.

Sadly, while this is yet another example of the often baffling extremes that London frequently throws in our faces, it's not a problem that's exclusive to London. It does, of course, exist in many other major cities around the world too, although judging by the obvious riches in the Kingdom of Fitzrovia, lack of money doesn't appear to be the fundamental issue.

With that in mind I head back towards Goodge Street station which is still illuminated by the brightness of the BT Tower, and I'm all ready to leave Fitzrovia. As I zigzag in and out of the shadows, Ralph McTell's classic 'Streets of London' pops into my head and I inadvertently find myself humming it as I'm walking along. I'm sure that when he wrote the song, way back in 1969, he couldn't possibly have foreseen that all these years later the lyrics would be just as relevant and poignant, and that the solitary characters shuffling around the lonely, cold-hearted streets in their ragged clothes would still exist, and still have little sign of pride in their eyes.

Rock & Stroll

And much less could he have imagined writing additional lyrics for this Ivor Novello Award winning masterpiece, but in 2020 he penned a powerful new verse in the wake of the Covid-19 pandemic. These latest words remind us of the desperate situation many homeless people have to contend with, but are also tinged with hope for a better show of human kindness in response to this virus and its indiscriminate nature that has no respect for wealth or position.

All of which puts me in a rather sombre and reflective mood as I hurry through the tube station entrance ready to start my journey home. The rain has been getting heavier and I'm getting wetter, but it's been another fascinating day of nostalgia, sight-seeing, people watching and earworms. And as Ralph McTell starts another chorus in my head, I feel more thankful than ever that at least I have a home to travel back to.

Chapter 10
Rock of Ages

Trekking into London for another day of delving into its musical past and I am once again reminded just how much I despise crowded trains and wonder how on earth people manage to put up with them on a daily basis.

Today hasn't been that bad either, I guess, as the trains have run pretty much to time and I even managed to get a seat on the train from Bedford, which is one of the advantages of living in a town that lies at the very end of the Thameslink line into London. Actually, I think it might be the only advantage. But even then a seat is never guaranteed and many people spend their daily commute into the big city by standing up every inch of the way. I take my hat off to them, but I draw the line at giving them my seat as well because I have another lot of walking to do today and they're nearly all younger than me anyway. I just hope they get well paid for it, because there's no amount of London weighting allowance that would persuade me to do this every day.

Having arrived at St. Pancras station, I take the Piccadilly Line to South Kensington and this time the commuters get their own back as I stand the whole way, crushed up against people so tightly I'm not sure if I breathed at all during the entire journey. It's amazing how

Rock & Stroll

long you can hold your breath when your face is tucked into someone else's armpit.

When I emerge from the station I take in lungfuls of air, grateful that even London's polluted offering smells as fresh as a field of daisies after a rush hour ordeal. Fortunately, South Kensington is one of the wealthiest, ergo one of the cleanest, parts of London, and its wide thoroughfares allow ample breathing space. It's a lovely morning too, bright, clear and sunny, meaning that at least this time Donovan has got the weather forecast right.

This does appear to have been a bit of a theme with Donovan, as following on from the songs 'Sunny Goodge Street' and 'Sunshine Superman' he released 'Sunny South Kensington' on the 1967 album 'Mellow Yellow', presumably while going through a phase of wanting to be a TV weather presenter. This track sees him taking a walk along Cromwell Road accompanied by a predictably psychedelic soundtrack, spreading his wings and tripping-out to the groovy raz (??) scene, along with several other hippy references that place the song firmly in the mid 1960s.

This was also about the time he was arrested in a high-profile drugs bust when a knock at the door of his Edgware Road flat resulted in several burly drug squad officers barging in. During the ensuing ruckus Donovan allegedly did what anyone else would have done in that situation, and jumped naked onto a policeman's back. All of which gives me considerably less faith in his weather forecasting abilities as I suspect his predictions of constant sunshine have somewhat more to do with pharmacology than meteorology.

From South Ken tube station I continue up the impressive Exhibition Road, named after The Great

Rock & Stroll

Exhibition of 1851 that was held in nearby Hyde Park and still home to many nationally important institutions to this day. These include the Victoria and Albert, Natural History and Science museums, the Royal Geographical Society and Imperial College, all of which guarantee a constant stream of visitors to the area, helped by a recently introduced shared space scheme that restricts traffic and allows greater freedom for pedestrians. This has undoubtedly enabled the spacious boulevard to show off its grand architectural mix of old and new in a far less cluttered manner, though many doubts still exist about the wisdom of allowing vehicles and pedestrians to mix quite so freely, as it is hard to be sure exactly where the pavement ends and the road begins.

It all seems to be working pretty well this morning though and the buildings look mightily impressive too, but I have to say the most fascinating exhibit I think I'll see down here today is the well tanned young man who just swaggered past me. He's sporting a Hagrid beard, a pair of yellow canvas deck shoes and a bright red and yellow shirt which displays the badge of Partick Thistle Football Club. You don't see many of those down here, and it's great to see this dis-located follower of fashion adding such a colourful thread to London's rich tapestry.

Shortly before reaching the end of Exhibition Road I turn left onto Prince Consort Road, one of the most expensive residential addresses in the UK and central to this area known affectionately as Albertopolis, in honour of Queen Victoria's husband. There are lots of memorials around here that recognise his commitment to establish this as a cultural district to celebrate science, the arts and education, with the most famous of these being, of course,

Rock & Stroll

the Royal Albert Hall, which itself has staged many huge rock and pop concerts over the years.

Leading from the south side of the Albert Hall down into Prince Consort Road is a hugely impressive set of stone steps which give a terrific view of the concert hall, making this all feel very regal. And in keeping with the royal theme, about halfway along the road is a plaque on the wall of the Imperial College Union Hall that marks one of the most iconic events in rock music history. For it was here, on 18th July 1970, that Queen played their first ever live gig in London, and where Freddie Mercury, Brian May, Roger Taylor and their original bassist Mike Grose (John Deacon joined shortly afterwards) took to the stage and started getting really noticed. Entrance to this event, staged at Brian May's alma mater, cost the paltry sum of 30p which sounds like a great bargain even then, let alone now that we know the significance of the occasion.

The commemorative plaque is very tasteful and clearly worshipped by all those who visit to pay homage to one of the world's best loved bands, but I have to say it's also extremely understated. Mounted high up to the left of an archway entrance and right by a bus stop it's quite easy to walk straight past it, which I very nearly did. Considering the extravagant influence that Queen, and especially Freddie Mercury, had on the world of music and entertainment, I must confess I was expecting something a little more flamboyant. Nonetheless, it's a deserved honour to be lauded in the grand surroundings of such an esteemed educational institution and is a great example of how time can change perceptions so much that a band once seen as wild and hedonistic cannot only be accepted,

Rock & Stroll

but positively treasured by the established order it once appeared to threaten.

As I turn left to leave Prince Consort Road onto the appropriately named Queen's Gate, I wonder to myself if we could ever see a band like them again. Music, as Queen themselves said in 'Radio Ga Ga', certainly does change through the years, but not always for the better, I'm afraid.

You've probably guessed this already, but I am not particularly a fan of modern chart music. In fact, on the whole, I think it's complete shite. There are admittedly still a few bands and the occasional solo artist that's worth listening to, but it's very rare. If you disagree with me, then I'm sorry, but I'm pretty confident that you do agree, otherwise you'd most likely have given up on this book by chapter 2 when you realised it's been written by someone with a totally different taste in music to yours.

Whenever I hear today's music - which is generally against my will - with its persistent bass thud, repetitive, unimaginative lyrics and lack of melody or musicality, it always feels lame, sterile and overproduced. This, I guess, is the result of record producers having been replaced by tech-savvy programmers who delight in swamping the airwaves with their superficial intelligence and annoying robotic samples that are so childish they sound as if they were laid down by Fisher-Price. And to finish it off, they create electronically enhanced, auto tuned vocal warbling specifically designed to just piss all over the backing track.

As for BBC Radio One, I'd rather have an earful of tinnitus than listen to the tuneless, irritating stuff they play nowadays. I simply don't get it and I have absolutely no desire to infiltrate their demographic either, but then I

Rock & Stroll

suppose that is the whole point of having song lyrics that are impenetrable to anyone over the age of twenty-eight. As far as I'm concerned, the music they play mostly has no guts, integrity or social conscience. It's repetitive, selfish and shallow, and seems to cover a very narrow range of subjects as they basically just sing about themselves, banging on relentlessly in the first-person about their whole self-obsessed, over-inflated idea of their own worth.

The songs I grew up listening to were raw, gritty and often rebellious. They dealt with social issues and political concerns, such as civil rights ('A Change is Gonna Come' and 'Happy Birthday'), anti war (What's Going On?), green issues ('Big Yellow Taxi'), transvestism ('Lola'), the privileged classes ('Eton Rifles'), obsessive stalking ('Every Breath You Take'), South African apartheid ('Free Nelson Mandela'), mass shootings ('I Don't Like Mondays'), urban decay ('Ghost Town'), unemployment ('One in Ten') and army youth recruitment policies ('Oliver's Army'). Back then, in order to make it in the music business you needed to have an instrument and an idea; now it seems all you need is an ego and an app.

I know younger people could point to the fact that there were far too many joke records and oddities that used to do well in the charts, such as 'Agadoo', 'The Birdie Song', Timmy Mallett, Jive Bunny and Joe Dolce. But to them I say "Shaddap you face". Yes, I admit the good old days weren't always good, and yes, we did have to endure the likes of 'Ernie', 'Grandad', Orville, The Wurzels and songs about floral dances, funky gibbons and a long haired lover from Liverpool. But I like to think that we knew they were crap, they just added a bit of novelty value and appealed to a wider audience, something that Radio One's slavish adherence to a playlist doesn't allow. And at least we can still remember them, even after all this time. I wonder how much music from the 2020s, with the very odd exception, will still be remembered in fifty years time, let alone be revered.

Ooh, I feel better for getting all that off my chest. Call me a miserable old bastard if you want to (okay, you already have), but nothing splits the generations like music. I know that rant makes me sound like my dad who, for similar reasons, pretty much hated any music after the 1950s. And he was right, of course. But then so am I, because there's no doubt that as we mature our ears just don't get it any more. This causes them to block out new music and ensures that our musical taste is one of the few things that doesn't change as we get older, like our views on the best James Bond, the best Doctor Who or the best team of Blue Peter presenters. It is just another undeniable and irreversible symptom of early onset nostalgia.

Having been thoroughly consumed by my trance-like musings, I'm now struggling to find my next destination which I was expecting to see on the right-hand side as I carried on down Queen's Gate, but it appears to have been moved. This causes me much consternation as I to-and-fro down the bottom end of the street, and being unable to find my street atlas in my rucksack makes me even more agitated. Then, luckily, I see a policeman on foot, such a rarity these days that at first I thought it was a mirage. I don't know why he was walking, I almost asked if he'd lost his car, but resisted the temptation and instead just asked if he could give me directions to Elvaston Place.

He was a young, polite and well spoken graduate type who couldn't have been any more pleasant or helpful,

Rock & Stroll

a far plod from the old image of the London cops I loved watching on TV as a kid. This bobby was more Jack Vegan than Jack Regan and it was reassuring to see him out and about, disproving the theory that there's never a policeman around when you need one. He very kindly, and without mentioning what an idiot I was, told me that I'd passed it ages ago and would have to double back.

With my tail between my legs I retrace my steps across Cromwell Road and, sure enough, I soon find Elvaston Place, a broad street of terraced houses with impressive front porches that stretches along to Gloucester Road at its western end. Many of these multi-storey houses appear to be made up of residential flats but with several business premises and foreign embassies adding further prestige to the mix.

Elvaston Place also lends its name to a song by the self-effacing Scottish folk rocker Al Stewart, an artist often overlooked despite his fine pedigree. This is a man who, early on in his career, played at the very first Glastonbury Festival in 1970, was friends with John Lennon and Yoko Ono and also shared a flat with Paul Simon.

The song 'Elvaston Place' featured as the B-side of his single 'The News from Spain' which was released in 1972, four years before his biggest commercial success, 'Year of the Cat'. It is based on the real life break up he had from his then girlfriend and paints a very vivid picture of the life he lived, and then lost, in the run-down basement flat on Elvaston Place that they shared together. Typical of Al Stewart's confessional style, the lyrics convey a visually strong image of a fairly impoverished but happy life at the bottom of the stone steps that led down to the basement, and of cuddling by the fireside while looking out through tatty lace curtains and splintered window frames. Despite the shabby interior of the flat, his characteristically bright vocal delivery and jaunty arrangement make it sound like a pretty contented existence. Until, that is, she dumps him in the third verse, and then London suddenly becomes a much lonelier place. Why do stories of lost love, especially true stories, always make the best love songs?

Having got a good flavour of what Elvaston Place has to offer I return to Queen's Gate and then head east along Cromwell Road, across Exhibition Road, near where I started, and then continue on towards Knightsbridge. (Yes, I know I've gone round in a big circle and didn't plan this bit very well, but if you think you can do any better, come and give it a go!).

As I pass the magnificent frontage of the Victoria and Albert Museum - again, I have to emphasise how spectacular the architecture is around here - I manage to dodge a skinny looking guy who hurriedly comes zagging towards me before zigging off to the side and then narrowly missing a lamppost while not once looking away from his phone. He is dressed in desert camouflage army combat gear and boots, although judging by his skeletal appearance, spatial awareness and severe lack of motional discipline, I suspect the closest he's ever been to Camp Bastion is building a sandcastle on Margate beach.

Grateful to avoid any further near misses I arrive at the junction where Cromwell Gardens joins Brompton Road on its way to Knightsbridge, and once there I am greeted by the very impressive sight of my next destination: The large, neo-Baroque, Roman Catholic

Rock & Stroll

Church of the Immaculate Heart of Mary, or Brompton Oratory as it is incorrectly but more commonly and succinctly known. This grand building, fronted with a facade of fine Portland stone, topped with a vast dome and crowned with a golden cross is as beautiful as it is imposing. Dating back to the 1880s, it is the second largest Catholic church in London (after Westminster Cathedral) and houses a colourful and intricately detailed Italianate interior adorned with some wonderful marble and stone statues.

Honoured on record by Nick Cave and the Bad Seeds with the track 'Brompton Oratory', taken from their critically acclaimed 1997 album 'The Boatman's Call', this song is another composition of lost love, but unusually set against the backdrop of attending mass on the morning of the Pentecost.

Nick Cave, the tall and strikingly serious looking Australian, is known for his religiously inspired songwriting and he sings here in his deep baritone voice of allowing his mind to wander during the reading, which comes from Luke 24, before then spending the rest of the service daydreaming about the lady he's missing. He pays envious homage to the statues of the apostles in the church and wishes that he could join them so he no longer has to endure the painful loneliness of being absent from his loved one.

Quite different from much of his earlier, often angrier work, this is an intensely emotional piece with a hauntingly slow, almost morose tempo and a stripped back arrangement which gives it a solemn, hymn-like quality that makes for a very different kind of love song.

Rock & Stroll

Having admired the wonderful church architecture of Herbert Gribble and been moved by the spiritually compelling lyrics of Nick Cave, I leave Brompton Oratory to again re-trace my steps back to South Kensington underground station, hopeful that my next tube ride will be more comfortable than my last. Once there, I head down to the District Line platform and pass one of the generally excellent buskers that entertain travellers on the network, and this one is no exception as he sings a superb rendition of Bob Marley's 'Redemption Song'. It sounds great on his smart Ovation electro-acoustic guitar and benefits even further from the surround sound experience provided by the arched walkway. I smile broadly as I drop a £2 coin into his guitar case and the noise of it hitting the other loose change startles him into opening his eyes, so lost was he in the song that they were closed tight as I approached. He nods in appreciation as I carry on by while humming along to his take on this classic song, which just happens to be one of my own personal favourites.

Obviously not all music can be to everyone's taste but, as the poet William Cowper famously wrote in 1785, "Variety is the very spice of life". That's most definitely true where music is concerned as a good blend of spices is essential to enrich the lavish feast we experience during our lives, and through my mental ramblings and musical memories I've experienced plenty of variety this morning. From the familiar, comforting sounds of 'Radio Ga Ga' and 'Redemption Song' to the bittersweet poignancy of 'Elvaston Place' and 'Brompton Oratory'. Add to the mix some tantalising psychedelia from Donovan and these have all blended well to spice up the insipid taste that was

Rock & Stroll

left in my mouth by the merest thought of some modern tunes that I simply can't stand.

This diverse array ensures that whatever your particular taste might be, whether similar to mine or poles apart, music can never be boring. Or, as William Cowper far more eloquently put it: "As the mind is pitched, the ear is pleased."

Rock & Stroll

Chapter 11
What a North and South!

From South Kensington I travel out west towards Fulham Broadway which is just a handful of stops and a quick clatter away on the District Line. Yet despite the short distance of the train journey there is still ample time for a couple of things to become hugely apparent to me. Firstly, I am one of very few passengers not using my phone. To be honest, I still prefer to people watch - mainly for fun, partly for my own personal safety and partly because my mobile phone usage is still somewhat limited by my poor grasp of technology. I never really thought mobiles would catch on so I didn't bother learning too much about them, and now they're so flipping complicated that I just don't stand a chance. My daughter often takes the mickey out of me, but I console myself that one day she might have children of her own and they will laugh at her aged inability to grasp the concept of driverless cars. Then she'll know how it feels.

As we pull into the station, the second thing that dawns on me is that I must be about the only person in the carriage without a tattoo or piercing. They're everywhere, on hands, arms, feet, necks, temples, ears, noses, cheeks. And that's just the visible ones - Lord knows what else they've got hidden away. Even though I've seen them all

Rock & Stroll

on display I still have absolutely no inclination to get one myself, but I can't help wondering why we struggle to recruit blood donors in this country when so many of the population appear to be obsessed with having their skin punctured by needles.

Having realised how much I must stand out due to my ordinariness it's quite a relief to leave the carriage and blend back into the wider world, which for me begins at Fulham Broadway underground station. This was recently refurbished to a very nice modern standard that now contains a cinema complex and food hall, but while being upgraded the old station building wasn't totally forgotten and still retains some of its original features, which themselves appeared in the 1998 rom-com 'Sliding Doors', starring Gwyneth Paltrow and John Hannah. It is probably even better known however, for the name-check it received on Ian Dury's 1978 hit 'What a Waste', in which he sang about career options that are more favourable than being a singer in a six-piece band. One suggestion, and the most frequently remembered, was being the ticket man at Fulham Broadway station, which is a fellow you don't see very many of these days.

In actual fact you don't see any of them at all, as they now have the job title of 'Customer Service Assistant' which certainly wouldn't have scanned so well in the song. But I'm sorry to say the one I see on duty today looks as if he would rather be anywhere other than here and responds to my smiling at him as I pass through the ticket gate like I'd just pissed all over his chips. If it's true that it takes more muscles to frown than it does to raise a smile, then this guy clearly thinks it's worth all the extra effort. To be fair though, this is pretty rare as most of the ones that I've

Rock & Stroll

seen usually look surprisingly cheerful. Maybe this one is just sick of people humming 'What a Waste' at him as they flash their Oyster card at the barriers.

To be honest, it's difficult not to because it's a very catchy tune and especially memorable for me too, as it was the first Ian Dury song I can ever remember hearing, and I absolutely loved it. That led to me buying his albums and Ian Dury and the Blockheads becoming one of my very favourite bands throughout my teenage years. I especially enjoyed their unruly attitude, the swearing in their lyrics and all the other rude things they sung about. What fourteen-year-old boy wouldn't like that?

But it wasn't just the swearing. That was only a part of some extremely clever, quirky, gritty and humorous lyrics that were delivered as a form of street poetry, and all very London-centric in character, subject matter and guttural vocal style as he brought his East End upbringing to life in music. Ian Dury was a great wordsmith who came up with some wonderfully ingenious rhymes, my own personal favourite being from the 1984 song 'Peter the Painter' in which he effortlessly rhymes "Royal Academy" with "Jack the Lademy."

'Peter the Painter' was written for his great friend and former tutor at Walthamstow School of Art, the world renowned artist Sir Peter Blake, a man himself synonymous with pop art having designed the cover for The Beatles' classic 'Sergeant Pepper' album. Dury himself went on to study at the Royal Academy of Art, hence he was also an excellent artist before deciding to concentrate on his music career. And in his lyrical songwriting and ear for native London lingo you can really hear the colourful

Rock & Stroll

vibrancy and originality of pop art shining through, like a kind of Hockney rhyming slang.

Ian Dury's appearance also fascinated me. As a teenager, I'm not sure how aware I was that he'd suffered from polio as a child, but I could see there was something about his look that made him different, and indeed his whole attitude had me engrossed. He was an improbable looking rock star, but his animated performances and captivating presence were able to draw people into his on-stage persona. There was a music hall theatricality about his sharp, witty and obscure lyrics which, coupled with his uneasy, hobbling gait and onstage tomfoolery, put me in mind of a mischievous character akin to a cross between the Joker, the Riddler and the Penguin, Batman's arch enemies, all rolled into one.

As I matured the lure of their swearing and sometimes crude innuendo lost its appeal, so I fell out of love with Ian Dury and the Blockheads in my very late teens. I rediscovered them in my thirties however, prompted by the release of their 'Mr Love Pants' album, when I realised there was a great deal more to their music than potty mouthed lyrics. Finding fame in the late 1970s I suppose it's inevitable they were labelled as a punk band and so their musicality was largely overlooked at the time. But when it came to music, the Blockheads certainly didn't live up to that name and their playing was far better than I was able to appreciate when I was younger, with very strong jazz, funk and reggae influences. The classic line-up of Charlie Charles (drums), Mick Gallagher (keyboards), John Turnbull and Wilko Johnson (guitars), Chaz Jankel (guitar and keyboards), Norman Watt-Roy (bass) and Davey Payne (sax) made the Blockheads a first

Rock & Stroll

rate band. These guys could seriously play, and with Chaz Jankel at the forefront as Ian Dury's main songwriting partner they knew how best to augment his lyrics with some amazingly rich and complex musicianship. If you want proof as to just how good they were, I suggest you listen to their skilful playing throughout 'Hit Me With Your Rhythm Stick', especially Watt-Roy on bass.

Ian Dury sadly died of cancer in March 2000, but despite being poorly with the disease was able to hit the road with the Blockheads shortly before he passed away. During this brief tour I was fortunate enough to see them play at Cambridge Corn Exchange and it was a dream come true for me to see one of my teen idols produce an amazing performance that belied how unwell he was. In his regrettable absence, I'm pleased to say the Blockheads still tour occasionally, ensuring Ian Dury's wonderful legacy lives on.

Still unable to witness a smile from the ticket man, I emerge from the tube station into wonderfully bright sunshine and begin heading east along Fulham Road. I am greeted almost immediately by Stamford Bridge and its hotel complex which is, of course, the world famous home of Chelsea Football Club, even though its location might have made the name Fulham F.C. more logical. Fulham's ground is some distance away however, beside the Thames near Putney Bridge, although still close enough for these well-to-do geographical neighbours to share an inextricable link that ensures a fierce rivalry between the two football clubs.

In terms of chart success between these age-old adversaries, Chelsea easily win that particular local derby having scored a big hit record in 1972 with 'Blue is the

Rock & Stroll

Colour', which reached number five in the charts just before that year's League Cup final. But on the field they weren't so lucky, as they went and lost 2-1 to Stoke City.

Chelsea's loss however, was also music's loss, as the tune was never going to win any songwriting trophies either, being a dreadful reminder of the days when football teams always used to release a single in the build up to a cup final. It was quite common for them to do well in the charts too, even though they were always awful. But don't tell that to any Chelsea fans, because it's still the club's signature tune to this day as well as being arguably the best known of all the cup final records ever made.

Most of my previous visits to this area have actually been football related as I often used to watch Fulham play at their home stadium of Craven Cottage, the oldest football league ground in London (as the state of their toilets could testify). This was mainly during the late 1980s when Fulham were perennial underachievers, seemingly destined to languish forever in the lower divisions. But I regularly went along with a good friend of mine called George, a larger-than-life character who was always jovial despite being a lifelong Fulham fan, and he seemed to appreciate me keeping him company in what was usually back then a near empty stadium.

Most of the games I saw were pretty dull, I honestly can't recall many goals being scored, and the highlight was generally a Wagon Wheel and a cup of Bovril at half-time. One memory does stay with me however, and even though it's not music related, it is far too good a story to not retell in this book.

In the days before the Premier League existed and footballers weren't millionaires, they would generally have

Rock & Stroll

a drink after the game in the player's lounge and this gave a few lucky fans the chance to rub shoulders with their heroes while standing at the bar. On one occasion, following a game against a team whose name I can't remember, George and I were having a quick drink in the lounge when he spotted ex-Fulham, but at that time current Manchester United and England defender Paul Parker. George wanted to ask for his autograph but took a while to pluck up the courage to approach him. I had an idea United were playing that night and so thought it surprising that Paul Parker would be here, at Craven Cottage, but by now George had gone and was standing at his side.

Nervously, he struck up a conversation with his hero before offering him a pen, and the autograph was duly signed. Then George, clutching it with delight, looked down at the signature, and quickly back at the player. "Who the fuck are you?!" he protested, thus ruining the proud moment that a young Charlton Athletic reserve player named Mickey Bennett signed what could well have been his first ever autograph.

Continuing along Fulham Road makes me wonder if Morrissey may also have joined us as an occasional spectator at Fulham, as his 1997 song 'Maladjusted', taken from the album of the same name, mentions a Stevenage overspill stretching into the night under the lights of Fulham Road. Could this be a reference to crowds leaving the ground, which is situated on Stevenage Road? The fact that the song begins with mention of a glorious defeat before progressing into a characteristically dramatic and despondent narration provides further confirmation of my suspicions that he was no stranger to the terraces at Craven

Rock & Stroll

Cottage. This would also explain his innate pessimism and profound misery, something I can definitely relate to from my time watching Fulham.

Further down Fulham Road, just by the entrance to the private cul-de-sac of Billing Road, stands The Fox and Pheasant pub which has been owned by singer-songwriter James Blunt since 2018. He apparently serves behind the bar on occasions, and while this charming country pub in a city setting is seriously tempting me, I decide to give it a miss as I don't know where my next toilet stop might be. So instead I turn right a little way before the pub and enter Maxwell Road, moving away from Arthur Daley's old manor around Fulham to venture further into the exclusive district of Kensington and Chelsea. This despite almost being put off by Elvis Costello's insistence that this was a place he didn't want to go to.

On their 1978 single '(I Don't Want To Go To) Chelsea', Elvis Costello and the Attractions were quite clear how they felt about the area, although having listened to the song many times I'm still not entirely sure why. The lyrics talk about fancy tricks and flirting, and of models waddling around in mini-skirts, all of which sound like pretty good reasons to have visited back in those days, before anyone had thought of political correctness. I guess I'm missing something, probably to do with the men in white coats that get mentioned halfway through, but either way it's still a fantastic song and a great example of lyrics that are open to interpretation depending on the imagination of the individual listener.

Anyway, whatever it was that so repelled the Attractions, it certainly didn't put Jon Bon Jovi off visiting the area before offering up his own darkly observational

Rock & Stroll

piece titled 'Midnight in Chelsea'. Written during a stay in London, it features on his 1997 solo album 'Destination Anywhere' and mentions such iconic symbols as Sloane Rangers and Routemaster buses. Strangely though, the video for the single was actually filmed once he'd arrived back in the USA and shot around the Chelsea neighbourhood of Manhattan, rather than the London version which inspired the song. So while Elvis Costello didn't want to go to Chelsea in the first place, it sounds as if Jon Bon Jovi, having visited, wasn't particularly keen on going back there either.

At the end of my short wander along Maxwell Road I turn left to head along the world famous King's Road - or maybe that should be Kings Road? It's difficult to know for certain as it changes depending on whichever street sign you look at. What does a possessive apostrophe matter anyway?

Well, quite a lot actually, especially if you happened to be King Charles II. Because this was his own personal road that he had built to connect Westminster to Hampton Court, and he'd only let you use it if you had a special pass. On maps and street atlases these days, as well as the majority of road signs, the apostrophe is inserted and generally accepted as being correct. So although it ceased being an exclusively royal road in 1830 and has been open for anyone to use ever since, including no doubt several other kings, Charles II still retains a hold over it. And being situated in the Royal Borough of Kensington and Chelsea, there is a notable air of exclusivity about King's Road that comes not only from its royal history, but from its more recent past as well.

Rock & Stroll

For this lengthy road that runs through the heart of Chelsea, connecting Fulham to Sloane Square, had long been renowned as a location for socialising and the arts, but then found itself at the forefront of Swinging London during the 1950s and '60s when it became world famous for being populated by many trend-setting boutiques and bazaars. To this day, the name is still synonymous with the ultra-modern and often outrageous fashions of the time. Vidal Sassoon, Twiggy, Mary Quant, Vivienne Westwood and Malcolm McLaren all made their mark up here, and that reputation for contemporary style and popular culture continued through the 1970s and '80s when punk, and then the Sloane Rangers, were in vogue. More recently still, the 'Made in Chelsea' social set have managed to keep the King's Road glitz and glamour alive in the minds of the reality TV viewing public.

Being right at the heart of fashion and pop culture naturally means King's Road also has strong links to the music industry and a range of artists as diverse as Sham 69, Generation X, Nazareth, Razorlight, 10cc and Al Stewart have all recorded songs that mention the place.

Unfortunately though, the ditty that chooses to pop into my head at this moment is the one penned in 1969 by the 'Carry On' film actor and sometime singer-songwriter Jim Dale, which was subsequently a hit for Des O'Connor. 'Dick-a-Dum-Dum (King's Road)' is often overlooked as a song about London, partly because of its inane title but mainly due to its storyline that sees the singer touring the city before returning to King's Road in the chorus to pick up some nice, shy, random girls. It is, as they say, a song of its time, and despite being undeniably catchy it is

Rock & Stroll

certainly not the street's finest moment, nor anyone else's for that matter.

Throughout the years many other rock and pop stars have shopped, worked and lived around King's Road, or been seen and photographed visiting its various haunts. Indeed, as I walk away from the Fulham end of the street one of the first sights I see to my left is Pimpernel and Partners furniture store. Specialising in classic, vintage and shabby chic furnishings, the wonderful old style frontage of this shop was captured for the cover of Mumford & Sons' 2009 debut album 'Sigh No More' which showed the members of this London-based folk rock quartet on display in the shop window. It is a very stylish yet understated image that naturally draws many passers-by to also stop and pose for a photo themselves.

Being nearly two miles long King's Road has a varied and architecturally diverse character with many elegant, unique, quirky and snazzy shops and restaurants mixing seamlessly with offices and residential properties, though all clearly affluent. So not surprisingly, it would be very easy to walk past the modest facade of number 484 without giving it a second glance, despite it once having been the headquarters of Led Zeppelin's management company, Swan Song, who also looked after The Pretty Things, Bad Company and Dave Edmunds.

A little further on and you reach the Worlds End clothing boutique, demurely standing a little way back from the tree adorned pavement yet strikingly bold in appearance. With its giant 13-hour wall clock with hands that move backwards, deceptively small front door, crooked tiling and a curious turquoise paint job that makes it look for all the world like a scene from 'Alice in

Rock & Stroll

Wonderland', this quaint exterior belies a powerful past. For rather than being a work of fantasy from the mind of Lewis Carroll, this is where the hard, rebellious reality of Vivienne Westwood's imagination created, along with her then partner Malcolm McLaren, an alternative clothes shop that offered a stark antidote to glam rock and pretty much everything else that was going on in the 1970s.

First opening as Let It Rock, a boutique that predominantly sold teddy boy and 1950s themed clothing, the store changed its name as Westwood brought out daring new fashion collections. And as their wares become more outrageous, so did the name of the shop, at first becoming Too Fast to Live Too Young to Die, then Sex, and then Seditionaries. This spirit of subversion and anarchy, along with its shocking and scandalous clothing, made it increasingly popular with the often disaffected youth of late 1970s Britain, while at the same time placing it hugely at odds with the traditional fashions associated with King's Road.

But, as they say, all publicity is good publicity, and the more cutting edge the shop became, the more the punters flooded in. Attracted by the lure of Vivienne Westwood's bold and provocative designs, the shop helped to create a new image for King's Road that was at the very heart of the punk rock revolution. For, although some would dispute it, this shop is often credited as being the birthplace of punk. Not just the fashions but also the music too, as the Sex Pistols, arguably the first and certainly the most notorious punk band, derived from here. Formed from members of the shop's staff, including Sid Vicious, and a couple of their regular customers, the most infamous

Rock & Stroll

being Johnny Rotten, Malcolm McLaren then managed the Pistols throughout their brief but controversial existence. As punk rock died out after just a few short years the name of the shop was changed again, this time to Worlds End, and it retains that title to this day, along with the non-conformist merchandise and quirky appearance that reflects its iconic history. And that sense of perversity even extends to its name, for unlike King's Road and the World's End pub that it's named after, the shop has no possessive apostrophe, which suggests a final galactic apocalypse at sometime in the near future.

With that in mind, it's worth noting that the World's End pub also gave its name to a local housing estate of 1960s tower blocks which was home for a while to Joe Strummer of The Clash. It was during his time living there that he was inspired to write 'London Calling', another prophesy of doom which, despite being a great song, gives you the idea that this perhaps wasn't the most cheerful part of Chelsea to inhabit. Having said that, it did look quite jolly in the street scenes for the video to Bob Marley's 'One Love/People Get Ready' which were shot along King's Road and on the World's End Estate itself.

Walking further along King's Road towards Sloane Square the more retail begins to dominate and there are plenty of smart and fancy clothing stores, although there's one I recall from my younger days that is no longer present. For it was around here, just after the curve near Park Walk, that I visited a clothes shop back in the early 1990s and, having taken a butcher's in the window, was tempted in by a pair of black leather trousers that were on display. Selfishly seduced by the idea of buying something so decadent on one of the trendiest shopping streets in the

Rock & Stroll

world, I took them to the fitting room and tried them on before realising what I should already have known - they made me look like a total dick.

I suppose the individualistic, expensive and sometimes just plain weird fashions of King's Road were never really meant for someone like me, and these often radical extremes of vogue are addressed by Tom Petty and the Heartbreakers on a 1981 song that they named in honour of the street. Included on their album 'Hard Promises', Tom Petty casts an amusing view over some of the street's past fashion excesses as he watches people wearing funny clothes (did he see me with those leather trousers?) and in the end opines that it's hard for a new world boy to shop for clothes on the old King's Road.

Nearing the end of my stroll along King's Road, I can't help concluding that while it is still a fashionable place to shop and be seen, the trendy image of its past is now somewhat outweighed by the reality of its present. This is similar to what I found on Carnaby Street, although King's Road seems to have adapted the better of the two as it still has a vibrancy that attracts a wealthy and stylish clientele in search of bygone classics, rather than Carnaby Street's inquisitively sentimental tourists seeking snippets from the past. But it has to be said that nowadays they are both being trounced in the trendy stakes by Camden.

Directly opposite Chelsea fire station I turn right to make my way along Oakley Street, stopping about halfway down at number 42 to look at the British Heritage blue plaque dedicated to Bob Marley. For it was while staying at this classy looking four-storey terraced house in 1977 that he and The Wailers recorded their iconic album 'Exodus'. And while not working in the studio, Bob

Rock & Stroll

reputedly spent most of his spare time playing his beloved football a short distance across the river in Battersea Park. Just imagine walking through the park and seeing Bob Marley stick one into the back of the net.

Among a diverse assortment of other notable people that have lived in Oakley Street through the years are David Bowie, polar explorer Robert Falcon Scott, Russian spy Donald Maclean and Oscar Wilde, who apparently lived in the same house as George Best, though obviously not at the same time.

At its end, Oakley Street opens out onto the wonderfully wide expanse of Chelsea Embankment and offers delightfully unobstructed views across the Thames. To turn right, or as those of a nautical persuasion would say "upstream" (stop me if I'm getting too technical), would take me the short walk to the spot where Fairport Convention guitarist Richard Thompson posed for the cover of his 1983 solo album 'Hand of Kindness'. The black and white photo of him in a raincoat holding his guitar with Battersea Bridge in the background looks a tad gloomy if I'm honest, and another song from this location, 'Chelsea Embankment' by Nikki Sudden and the Jacobites, doesn't lift the mood very much either, as it somberly tells of unrequited love in the rain. It is beautifully sung though by female vocalist Max Edie, aka Lizard, whose crisp tones, reminiscent of Kirsty MacColl, also adorned The Waterboys' massive 1980s hit 'The Whole of the Moon'.

Rather than wander along Chelsea Embankment to see more of this location, I choose to cross Old Father Thames via the historic Albert Bridge which is undoubtedly one of the most picturesque bridges across the river. Designed by R.M.Ordish and opened in 1874 to

Rock & Stroll

ease the increasing burden on Battersea Bridge, over the years it too became victim of heavier than planned usage leading to the threat of demolition in the 1950s as it was deemed to have become structurally unsound. It was reprieved after a campaign waged primarily by future poet laureate John Betjeman, and as a result its original suspension design was strengthened and a weight limit imposed to reduce traffic flow. Although being more stable nowadays, its long disused toll booths still bear signs warning troops from the old Chelsea Barracks to break step while crossing the bridge in order to avoid it wobbling under the strain of their marching boots.

An additional danger more recently posed to the structure of the bridge, specifically the timbers that under-pin its deck, has come from a very unlikely source. Apparently they've been slowly rotting away after years of having dogs urinating against them on their way to and from walkies in Battersea Park. Not the greatest accolade for the bridge I suppose, nor to Prince Albert whose idea it was to build a toll crossing here in the first place.

While it may not be the sturdiest structure across the Thames, the Albert Bridge is definitely one of the most enchanting, its brightly painted framework giving it a clean and uncluttered look in contrast to some of its dowdy cousins that span this stretch of the river. The design was based upon the Franz Joseph Bridge in Prague and it definitely has a continental look about it. At night-time it is tastefully illuminated, again in keeping with this stylish part of London, and John Betjeman himself described it as "one of the beauties of the London River."

As I cross the bridge, I am struck by how exposed it seems and this allows a refreshing breeze to pass

Rock & Stroll

through its latticework of structural supports, making a very pleasant change from the claustrophobic clag of the big city. The views up and down the river are stunning, helped by its broad width at this point and also due to it being far enough away from Central London to be lined primarily with trees rather than imposing architecture.

So it's no wonder that Albert Bridge has provided inspiration for several songwriters over the years, from a suitably uplifting track by musician/producer Ribside, featuring Nick Heyward, to a depressing one from post-punk outfit The Monochrome Set which includes Albert Bridge as a possible place for suicide. But the view from here is far too life-affirming to dwell on that, so I'll swiftly move on and mention my own favourite offering: 'Misty Morning, Albert Bridge', by The Pogues.

Released as a single in 1989, it tells of a dream that ends with two separated lovers meeting up again in the morning mist by the bridge. Set against the typical Irish folk/punk sound of The Pogues, the song has such an eerily calm mood you can just imagine the bridge supports being shrouded in a swirling haze, with its tasteful illuminations making it a beautiful sight. And this can be viewed in the video to The Pretender's 'Don't Get Me Wrong' where Chrissie Hynde struts across the bridge at twilight.

I'm now more than halfway across the bridge and with each step I can feel a growing sense of trepidation as I am also well on my way to arriving on the south side of the river, an entire area that I'm broadly unfamiliar with. Virtually all my visits to London through the years have been concentrated around the north, and with very little need to venture south my journeys over the Thames generally stalled on the South Bank. About the only

Rock & Stroll

exception was a six month stint during 2019 when I regularly visited at weekends while my daughter, Erin, attended theatre school at Elephant and Castle. I'm not sure how typical an example of South London life The Elephant actually is, but I'm afraid I didn't really like it very much. I can clearly remember its enormously imposing residential tower blocks and a ghastly outdated shopping centre that would have looked more at home in North Korea. While I confess it did manage to grow on me a little over those few months, and I always got a nostalgic thrill walking past the old corner shop in Brook Drive where the video for 'Come On Eileen' was shot, it still too often felt like it was on a different planet despite being in the same city that I was used to. And walking round during the dark winter evenings made me feel quite vulnerable at times as I couldn't help feeling that a significant number of the local population wanted to hurt me.

So now, as I leave behind the swirling, murky depths of the Thames that provide the border between North and South London, I decide to pull up my hood to try and hide the fact that I'm a bald, middle-aged, spectacle wearing tourist. I even find myself beginning to walk more upright and with a slight swagger too, in an attempt to appear less like a prospective mugging victim, but more like a mugger. According to most of the reports I've seen in the popular press and on media sites recently, south of the river is a seething hotbed of crime, so hopefully these changes of appearance will help me blend into this gangster's paradise that I'm about to enter.

Like Julius Caesar crossing the Rubicon, I am journeying into the unknown and there can be no turning back. Wish me luck.

Chapter 12
Pigs Might Fly

Although I've been putting off coming south of the river for as long as I can remember, I'm pleased to say that my initial impression leads me into thinking it might not be the dreadful experience I'd been anticipating after all, and that maybe the north-south divide isn't as big as it's often made out to be. Surprisingly, everything looks rather pleasant.

Those impressions are certainly helped by the fact that having crossed Albert Bridge I immediately enter the lush green expanse of Battersea Park, one of the jewels of London. The sun is still shining and just to the left of me, on the riverside pathway, is an elderly couple - I guess in their seventies - walking along slowly, hand in hand; a sight that always gladdens the heart. It really is quite lovely down here.

All of which makes me wonder why I've always had such an aversion to the south and why I'd not made more effort to visit Battersea Park previously. There certainly don't appear to be any muggers lying in wait for me and no crouching tigers or hidden dragons either - mind you, I haven't reached the petting zoo yet. Thinking back, probably the only time I've ever been here before was to visit the funfair when I was a young boy. In fact, I

Rock & Stroll

must have been very young as the fair shut down in 1974 following a terrible accident on the Big Dipper that tragically killed five children and injured another thirteen.

Apart from my vague childhood recollections of that disaster, I suppose my other preconceived ideas about Battersea Park were shaped by the fact that whenever I hear the name Battersea, I immediately think of just two things - either the dog's home or the power station. In my defence though, I suspect it's probably quite common for people of my generation to have that initial reaction, none of which, I'm afraid, suggests that the place is particularly welcoming or exciting.

Unless, of course, you happen to be a Pink Floyd fan, in which case the mere mention of the power station will generate a surge that'll send your particles positively buzzing. For this monstrously large and unattractive brick powerhouse featured on the front of their 1977 release 'Animals', leading it to become one of the most instantly recognisable album covers in music history.

Not that Pink Floyd are strangers to distinctive album covers, with the sleeves to 'Dark Side of the Moon', 'Wish You Were Here' and 'The Division Bell' all ranked as some of the most iconic of all time. And as with those, 'Animals' is an incredibly bold and powerful piece of art, even though appearing to be quite mundane and simplistic at first glance.

Conceived by founder member and bassist Roger Waters and designed by Storm Thorgerson, the cover design shows an inflatable pig flying between two of the power station's huge chimneys, portrayed against the backdrop of a smoky, industrial sky. To begin with it all looks quite bleak and oppressive as the presence of the flying pig is not immediately obvious, an oversight that rather diminishes the fun they had while taking the photographs that were to be used on the cover.

Bearing in mind these were the days before CGI and Photoshop, in order to bring the concept to life they had to commission a 12-metre high helium filled air balloon shaped like a pig and tether it between the two chimneys. During the shoot however, the balloon broke free of its moorings and drifted into Heathrow airspace causing flights to be cancelled as pilots reported seeing the low flying pig. It eventually touched down somewhere in Kent, apparently causing further panic to a field full of cows.

They certainly don't make album covers like that any more, which is yet another downside to the way music is packaged and promoted these days. A 12-inch record sleeve with an accompanying inner wallet gave huge scope for creating imaginative artwork to complement the music you were buying and enhance the entire experience. It seems strange to think this now, but during the vinyl years the picture sleeve was almost as important as the record itself, and I for one have bought many albums on the strength of a cover shot alone. I miss them so much.

Although no longer functioning as a power plant, a spruced-up Battersea Power Station is still in existence today but as a mixed use retail and residential enterprise. Indeed, much of the local district has undergone massive redevelopment over the past couple of decades which has seen the construction of a brand new United States Embassy building and two underground stations, at Nine Elms and Battersea, as an extension to the Northern Line.

Rock & Stroll

This local modernisation was the subject of a 2007 song by Welsh band Super Furry Animals called 'Battersea Odyssey' which bemoans the more crass elements of the power station's gentrification, as well as that of the surrounding area. But there's no doubt that it still strikes a mightily formidable pose as it stands over the Thames just past Chelsea Bridge, its magnitude made even more remarkable by the fact that it was designed by Sir Giles Gilbert Scott, the architect who also devised red telephone boxes; that's quite a jump in scale. Despite the enormity of the structure however, its position some distance away in Nine Elms means that it's not possible to see much of it from the side of the park that I'm walking along - parallel to Albert Bridge Road - largely because it's obscured by an impressive proportion of the eight million or so trees that grow all across London's parklands.

Aside from its foliage Battersea Park has many other attractions and amenities, including sports pitches, a bowling green, lakes with boats for hire, herb gardens, a Japanese Buddhist peace pagoda, cafes, a bandstand and a children's zoo. Pretty much something for every age group in fact, yet still the very youngest seem to prefer making their own entertainment, as I can see just ahead of me a couple of small children having a whale of a time jumping around in a big muddy puddle - that Peppa Pig has got a lot to answer for.

Then, as I'm nearing the adventure playground, an altogether much calmer and cleaner small boy gives me a massive grin and a wave as he walks past. As I smile back at him and his parents, I think how nice it would be if we didn't have to grow out of that delightful stage of innocence; if we could just smile and greet total strangers

Rock & Stroll

as they pass by, with no hidden agenda and no reason for them to feel threatened. How much of a better place the world would be for a simple bit of friendliness and goodwill. Oh well, one can only dream.

On leaving the park, I continue a little further along Albert Bridge Road before turning right onto Battersea Park Road and, as I'm walking, I reflect on a couple of other very moving songs connected to the area, namely 'Battersea Moon' by Eddi Reader and 'Battersea Boys' by Chris Difford. The latter of these, taken from Difford's 2008 solo album 'The Last Temptation of Chris', is a particularly poignant tale of childhood anguish and brotherly love that was written as a gift to a friend and is told in the empathetic and sensitive way you would expect from this masterful lyricist.

Along with his songwriting partner and fellow guitarist Glenn Tilbrook, Chris Difford was the driving force behind the massively successful group Squeeze, one of my all-time favourite bands. Led by these two Greenwich guys, with support from fellow members and astounding musicians such as Jools Holland, Gilson Lavis and Paul Carrack, Squeeze had umpteen hits from the late 1970s and throughout the 80s. Together they are responsible for several of the greatest songs of that period, with ridiculously catchy tunes and some of the cleverest lyrics ever to be written. Many of those songs take inspiration from their London roots and the band continues to tour to this day with Difford and Tilbrook at the helm, their individually distinctive yet mutually harmonic vocal styles still complimenting each other perfectly.

With Squeeze very much in mind I turn left to head down Falcon Road towards Clapham Junction, and even

Rock & Stroll

though it's still some distance away I can already feel a sense of excitement growing within me. Not because this is Britain's busiest railway intersection, with more lines running through it than you'd find on a Rolling Stones' face, but because it provided the title for what is possibly Squeeze's finest and undoubtedly one of the nation's favourite songs: 'Up The Junction'.

The fact that it shares this unromantic title with a play by Nell Dunn, a story of sixties social realism that was directed for TV by Ken Loach, is entirely fitting as this is a real kitchen sink drama of a song. In just three minutes it tells in vivid detail a story of young love, loss, pregnancy, poverty, alcoholism and smelly nappies, all based in and around the Clapham area.

'Up The Junction' was a massive hit which reached number 2 on the UK charts in 1979, but is an unusual composition for a hit record as it has no chorus and only mentions its title once during the entire song, and even then as the very last line. That Difford and Tilbrook's writing should be so bold as to create such a successful song in this unorthodox way and from so gritty a subject matter is a huge tribute to their skill as songwriters. It is rightly deserving of its popularity.

I've been walking quite a long time now so I'm very glad when Clapham Junction railway station finally comes into view, but equally sad to say that it's a bit of a let down in comparison to the song. From the road all I can see is a load of power cables running overhead and a huge iron bridge surrounded by blocks of flats. Not sure what else I was expecting really, I don't suppose it was ever likely there would be a big blue plaque mounted on the bridge declaring it to be the location of one of my

Rock & Stroll

favourite songs, but it might be nice if they cleaned up the pigeon shit once in a while. Perhaps the station looks better from one of the side roads, but at least now I can understand why, when they built the railway interchange in 1863, they named it Clapham Junction despite being geographically located in Battersea, as Clapham was seen as being more stylish. Clearly they felt it needed all the help it could get.

The dreary surroundings do give the song's lyrics some gritty realism though, which is more than can be said for a number released by Toyah Willcox in 1985 that takes its title from the name of the junction because, try as I might, I just can't work out what those lyrics are actually about. Musically, it is a typical Toyah post-punk track sung in her unmistakably urgent and dramatic style, but I'm afraid it really hasn't aged very well - sorry Toyah.

After passing under the railway bridge I arrive at a four-way road junction and take a look to the right where I can see the impressive red brick top of The Clapham Grand, a live music venue that has staged performances from a range of great artists including Chuck Berry, The Temptations, Madness and The Jam. The Kinks have also played there which is rather fitting because from here I turn left into Lavender Hill, a street that gives its name to a song that featured on their 1973 release 'The Great Lost Kinks Album'.

Although recorded in 1967 this song took six years to finally be released and is yet another example of Ray Davies' wistfully poetic writing style, using lyrics that conjure up a yearning for the simple, underestimated pleasures of life, like a Sunday afternoon walk and a nice cup of tea. In that regard it's similar in concept to some of

Rock & Stroll

The Kinks' other offerings, such as 'Autumn Almanac', 'We Are The Village Green Preservation Society' and 'Sunny Afternoon', although 'Lavender Hill' does have a darker, eerie, 'Strawberry Fields' vibe to it.

As well as being the subject of a Kinks song, Lavender Hill is probably more widely known in popular culture for the Ealing Studios comedy 'The Lavender Hill Mob', a 1951 classic movie which starred Alec Guinness as a local resident who hatches a plan to steal a consignment of gold bullion by melting it down into miniature souvenirs of the Eiffel Tower.

The street itself is a three-quarter mile long road that was greatly developed following the opening of Clapham Junction station, rapidly filling up with large residential properties and several major civic and commercial buildings, the most impressive being Arding and Hobbs. Opened in 1910, this was at the time London's biggest department store south of the Thames, an accolade that further added to the prestigious credentials of the locality. Many years later the store featured heavily in the video to The Human League single 'Life On Your Own', before going on to become a branch of Allders and then a Debenhams and now - well, who knows what?

Despite its past splendour it has to be said that the area does have a bit of a downmarket appearance to it nowadays, but I assume it's also pleasantly quirky as I see a middle-aged couple riding down the hill towards me on a tandem. At the risk of causing offence though, I can't help wondering if it's possible to ride a tandem without looking like a bit of a tit.

So while most of Lavender Hill's grand old buildings are still in existence, there's no surprise that many of them are occupied by the same businesses that populate most of our retail outlets nowadays. Coffee chains, restaurants, takeaways, convenience stores, hair, nail and tanning salons, vape shops, tattoo studios, estate agents and bookmakers all abound to make up the Great British shopping experience of the 21st century. No doubt some of those will be taking over parts of Arding and Hobbs in the near future too. And just to prove how little variation there is on today's shopping streets, at the crossroads where Lavender Hill becomes Wandsworth Road I turn right into Cedars Road and at this junction alone there are two coffee shops, a supermarket and a bookies.

While I reluctantly accept the changing face of retail as more and more shopping is done on the internet, and the inevitable decline of the traditional High Street this has caused, I have to say that I am most unpleasantly surprised at the huge influx of bookmakers there has recently been into retail premises. I know that gambling has been one of this country's most successful growth industries since the turn of the century, but as much of this is done online I wonder why there is such a need for local bookie's shops when you can just lose all your money in the comfort of your own home.

One racing certainty however, is that when I reach the end of the wide, tree-lined thoroughfare that is Cedars Road, it will bring me out directly opposite the picturesque scenery of Clapham Common. And sure enough, when it has done so, I pause to look out over this green and pleasant land which again reminds me of Squeeze's classic 'Up The Junction', the drama of the song having unfolded one windy night on this very common.

Rock & Stroll

The tale didn't stop there either, because in 1998 Squeeze released the song 'A Moving Story' which is a follow-up to the original, but heard from the woman's point of view rather than the man's, as was the case with 'Up The Junction'. Having loved the original song for as long as I can remember it's very interesting to hear how her life panned out after the two of them split up, although it does make me want to know more about what happened to him as well. (See Bonus Track, page 242.) But whatever he got up to, it's great that a song so beloved should have a sequel because this classic story thoroughly deserved to be revisited.

While looking out over the common, I smile to myself as I recall a favourite memory from when I saw Glenn Tilbrook playing a solo gig in the late 1990s at the marvellous Esquires venue in my home town of Bedford. It was a brilliant show with him performing most of Squeeze's greatest hits plus a few of his own solo compositions. But the real highlight of the show came about halfway through when he asked what Bedford was like on a Friday night and then, without further ado, led the couple of hundred or so members of the audience outside, against the wishes of the bouncers, and along the Bromham Road. Walking at the head of the group while playing 'Goodbye Girl' on his guitar, he led us the few hundred yards to The Blarney Stone pub. Once there, he wandered in and casually announced - "Hello, I'm Glenn Tilbrook from Squeeze" - whereupon he joined the local band playing the pub that night in a rendition of several Beatles' songs. The band's joy at playing an impromptu gig with one of the greats of British popular music was only surpassed by that of the pub landlord who managed to more than quadruple his night's takings in the twenty minutes or so we were there.

This entirely surreal experience was rounded off by Tilbrook again guiding us through the streets like the Pied Piper, leading us all in a chorus of 'Hey Jude' while cars slowed down to watch as they passed by. We then returned to Esquires where he continued his normal show as if nothing much out of the ordinary had happened.

Returning from this reverie that has had me standing still for the last few minutes, I take in more of the scenery that Clapham Common provides as yet another example of London's lush green parks. Consisting of 220 acres of grassland, its vast triangular form is today being enjoyed by numerous dog walkers, skateboarders, frisbee throwers, footballers and picnickers, all stretching as far as the eye can see. I also notice an events poster advertising an upcoming English Civil War re-enactment, although the armour-clad Roundhead featured in the picture looks more like Oliver Hardy than Oliver Cromwell. In addition to this skirmish the common contains various public sports facilities, playgrounds, three sizeable ponds and a grand Victorian bandstand which is the largest in London. It has also played host to several star-studded music festivals over the years.

In stark contrast to the exuberance of those festivals, the North Side road that borders the common, along which I'm now walking, found itself being used as the setting for a strange event that occurred in a 1991 song by Morrissey entitled 'Mute Witness'. In typically dramatic Morrissey fashion this track, set to an urgent and persistent piano beat, has some disturbing and sinister lyrics that upon first listen seem to be in keeping with some of the

Rock & Stroll

heavily publicised and unpleasant stuff that has happened on the common over the years. Digging deeper however, it actually appears to be about a young deaf girl who has seen a UFO on the common and is trying to explain what she has witnessed. So maybe not quite such a traumatic song as it originally seemed, though still not exactly celebrating the area either. But then I don't suppose we should be expecting anything less weighty or earnest from Morrissey.

Much more cheerful is the instrumental piece 'Clapham South' by British R&B/funk band Gonzalez, who were mentioned in a previous chapter with regard to the song 'Funky Frith Street'. Both these numbers featured on their eponymous 1974 album release, and this is a similarly upbeat tune but with a more Latin American dance feel to it that contains more notes than I ever thought was possible to get out of a flute.

North Side has now become Long Road and as I'm nearing the end, which will bring me to Clapham Common tube station, a young black man cycling quickly towards me falls off his Boris Bike and ends up in a right heap straddling the gutter. I rush across to him, anxious to check if he's okay. He says that he is, but he clearly isn't from the way he's struggling to haul himself and his bike back up onto the safety of the pavement. Pride is such a great anaesthetic.

I double check if he needs any assistance, but again he declines my offer of help while sitting on the grass verge and tending to his wounds. Though he's clearly a bit shaken and very embarrassed by the fact that several other passers-by, on foot and in cars, have now stopped to have

Rock & Stroll

a look, he doesn't want to show it or make a fuss, so I try to ease his embarrassment by making light of the situation.

"Don't worry", I say quietly. "I don't think anyone else noticed."

"Thanks, bro" he chuckles, and gives me a fist bump of gratitude.

Satisfied that he's well enough to not need my help I leave him to it and continue on, proud of myself for being the only person who offered him any assistance and for that brief moment of comradeship that saw a young black guy with short dreadlocks and a gold chain fist bump me, an uncool, middle-aged white man with balding grey hair and a backpack.

Approaching the tube station I see ahead of me one of my pet hates (okay then, one of my menagerie of hates). Two young men are walking towards me wearing white socks with sliders - or, as they used to be called, open toed sandals.

As anyone of my generation knows only too well, socks with sandals is a complete fashion no-no. Yet here we are in the 21st century and all because a few rappers and footballers decide to start wearing them, suddenly they're not only an acceptable combo but are positively trendy. Do these people not have mirrors in the house to see what an awful thing they've done to their feet? They can call them sliders all they want, but you can't hide the truth. I know an open toed sandal when I see one.

Fortunately, I've now arrived at the entrance hall to Clapham Common underground station which is far more aesthetically pleasing and cheers me up no end. This listed building made of light stone slabs has a charming dome shaped roof that's quite similar in style to that of the

Rock & Stroll

bandstand on the common and is adorned with a fringe of TfL corporate navy blue. The overall appearance is helped even more by the fact that it's situated next to a quaint clock tower in matching stone that looks like a giant stack of Jenga blocks, all of which makes this one of the most picturesque station exteriors on the entire network and fits beautifully with the cosmopolitan vibe at this end of the common.

This is now about the furthest south I've ever ventured in London, at least on foot, and although I've only been here for a short time, I confess to already being very pleasantly surprised by how pretty it can be and how much I'm enjoying myself. The sun is still shining, I've walked through two of London's biggest and most famous parks, I've made some new friends, albeit fleetingly, and all seems right with the world. I didn't think any of that would ever happen; in fact, I thought it was more likely that pigs could fly.

But since I've been south of the river, I've found out even that's possible too.

Rock & Stroll

Chapter 13
Eclectic Avenue

Moving along from Clapham Common, the next stage of my walkabout takes me down Clapham Park Road to journey further into these southern territories that are all quite new to me. At my current walking pace I am about, to quote the name of a song by Carter the Unstoppable Sex Machine, '24 Minutes From Tulse Hill'. I'm sure they won't mind me borrowing the title - after all, they did kind of scam it from Gene Pitney's '24 Hours From Tulsa' in the first place.

    Mind you, from the picture the song paints of Tulse Hill I don't think I'll bother heading down that way. In keeping with many of my pre-formed ideas about South London it does sound rather dark and threatening, and they should know because guitarist Les Carter is originally from Tulse Hill himself. However, considering their song dates back to 1998 I am still optimistic from what I've seen so far that South London has largely changed for the better since then.

    Nearing the end of Clapham Park Road I pop into a corner shop for a bottle of spring water to keep myself hydrated and to see if I can buy a small pair of scissors to cut out the label from the back of my shirt as it's irritating the hell out of me. Bloody thing. How come we can send a man to the moon, harness the energy of the sun, split the

Rock & Stroll

atom and recreate the effects of the Big Bang, yet we can't find a way of attaching a label inside a shirt without it itching like a bitch.

Disappointingly, they tell me they don't have any scissors so I buy a pack of sticking plasters instead, which I will use to protect the area on the back of my neck from being scratched any further. As I exit the shop I see a young, casually dressed African lady approaching and so I hold the door open for her. She is wearing a pair of hoop earrings so large it must take all her effort not to trip over them, but she still manages to give me a pleasant smile of thanks as she passes through the doorway.

Shortly after leaving the shop I cross Bedford Road and enter Acre Lane, another typically wide suburban thoroughfare with a mixture of retail and residential properties that will lead me even deeper into the Borough of Lambeth. Acre Lane shares its name with a marvellously catchy 2008 song by Brixton-based indie rock band The Thirst which, unlike Carter USM, manages to give a quirky, feel-good snapshot of some of the less appealing aspects of everyday life in South London, and along this street in particular.

Another quirky thing that makes me smile at this point is a builder's van I've just seen driving past with an eye-catching slogan on the side. I had to look twice to make sure I read it correctly and, for sure, it did advertise their services as: "Pavements, Driveways and Patois." So no doubt there's either a dyslexic local signwriter on the loose or a firm of cool Jamaican block pavers specialising in cultural dialect. I sincerely hope it's the latter as that would be a unique selling point, and a slogan to rank alongside my all-time favourite which I saw back in the

Rock & Stroll

1990s from a firm of Asian builders that read: "You've Tried All The Cowboys, Now Try The Indians."

As the end of Acre Lane draws nearer I am getting close to the centre of Brixton which is yet another part of the city I've never visited before, and I'm very conscious of one of the main reasons why. For anyone of my generation is well aware, the name Brixton will always be inextricably linked with the race riots of the 1980s, a sad chapter in the history not just of London but the entire country, and this has shaped many people's perception of the area ever since.

The first of these riots flared up in 1981 following a period of increased police activity, including a widespread stop-and-search operation, in response to a significant rise in the area's levels of street crime. This was perceived locally as being unnecessarily heavy handed and unfairly skewed against the sizeable black community. Tensions and mistrust had already been growing over a period of time, all of which culminated in rioting finally breaking out on April 10th that lasted for several days, with buildings being burned and petrol bombs, along with other missiles, being thrown at police in a display of violence that was beamed across the world. Hundreds of people were injured and in the ensuing days many other towns and cities saw copycat rioting and looting take place.

Like most people I found those images extremely sad and deeply shocking as I had never before witnessed anything like them in my own country, and even though the hostilities seemed to calm down for a while, there were further riots in 1985 and again in 1995 which further tarnished the reputation of the area.

Rock & Stroll

Although much progress seems to have been made since those riots, racism is depressingly still a major issue in London and in British society as a whole. Alarmingly, it even appears to be on the increase as various societal and political changes seem to have raised levels of ignorance and general intolerance within society. The fact that people can be so beastly to others due solely to the colour of their skin saddens me greatly, as it should any right-minded person. It also surprises me that while generations have moved on to a point where we all live, shop, work and go to school alongside each other, watch the same sports together and happily listen to and enjoy the same music, some people still have hatred, mistrust and resentment simmering away in their bigoted little hearts.

Being a middle-aged white man I can never know first hand the effects of racism. In fact, I can honestly say that I don't think I've ever experienced any significant degree of discrimination at all so I may be wrong or naive to say this, but music does seem to be one of very few aspects of modern British life that is relatively unaffected by racism. It has long displayed the acceptance and openness that a multi-cultural society should have and is accessible to all, regardless of race, creed, gender or sexual identity. Music is a diverse and powerful force for good, and long may that continue.

Due to the notoriety of Brixton's past I must confess that I'm quite nervous as to what I shall make of it when I get there, although from what I've read and heard I'm pretty confident it has moved on significantly from those dark days of the 1980s. Even so, some of the same issues of poverty and deprivation still remain and there are certain streets that may best be avoided, but I'm sure that's

Rock & Stroll

also the case with most other London boroughs, so it's not a problem exclusive to Brixton.

I do have a further hint of what to expect from modern-day Brixton due to a 2020 song by British-born Jamaican DJ, activist and reggae performer Macka B, which is called 'Gentrification'. This thought-provoking piece of social commentary documents the changing character of the area following the recent influx of more well-to-do residents and upmarket businesses. While this new money has improved Brixton in many ways, the song highlights the fact that this general increase in affluence has also resulted in the displacement of many long-term local residents, especially those of Afro-Caribbean descent, and a loss of community spirit.

One sign of affluence is very evident as I reach the end of Acre Lane, although this particular sight that greets me is certainly not the result of any recently acquired riches. The mightily impressive stone and brick structure of Lambeth Town Hall that wraps itself around this corner of Brixton Hill dates back to 1908 and dominates the local area with its tall clock tower that chimes on the quarter hour, while sculpted figures representing science, art, literature and justice keep watch over its four faces. It's a lovely piece of Edwardian Baroque style architecture and an absolute pleasure to look at.

Then, just across the road on the opposite corner, is another attractive Edwardian facade, this one fronting the popular Ritzy cinema and cafe bar which opened 1911 as one of Britain's earliest purpose built cinemas. Next door to this is the equally impressive looking but much more highbrow Brixton Library, built in 1893 and gifted to the borough by sugar tycoon Sir Henry Tate. This great

Rock & Stroll

benefactor who generously gave to many causes, often anonymously, is proudly commemorated with a bronze bust at the main entrance, which starts me wondering whether philanthropic acts of this nature still occur today. I certainly don't hear of any, at least not on this scale. How my local library would benefit from having a rich sugar daddy like Sir Henry Tate, instead of crossing their fingers in the hope of a more generous share of the council tax to avoid cutting services any further.

Next to the library, a short way across Windrush Square, is a much more recent and very significant addition to this selection of local places of interest. The Black Cultural Archives, which opened in 1981, is Britain's only national heritage centre dedicated to documenting, preserving and celebrating the history, achievements and people of Caribbean and African descent on these shores.

There is a marvellous atmosphere all around this corner of Brixton Hill this afternoon, as it's absolutely buzzing with a vibrant mix of people enjoying the assorted attractions. Unfortunately, the only blot on this charming and wonderfully historic landscape comes from the local branch of KFC, which is today fronted by various pieces of branded detritus and some discarded scraps of chicken strewn across the pavement. All very disappointing I'm afraid, as I would frankly have expected a far tidier and more disciplined appearance from a company that's run by somebody as high ranking as a colonel. It all looks finger-lickin' bad.

Having crossed the intersection I progress into Coldharbour Lane which runs the mile or so south-east towards Camberwell. As well as being one of the central hubs of the 1981 riots, it also has the dubious distinction of having been both the location of former Prime Minister John Major's childhood home and being suggested in a 2003 issue of the Evening Standard as possibly the most dangerous street in Britain.

Musically, Coldharbour Lane features in several songs, it's infamous reputation for drug dealing, after-hours drinking dens and general maverick behaviour making it a source of intrigue and inspiration for a range of songwriters including Procol Harum's Matthew Fisher, The Quireboys and Tom Robinson. Brixton band Alabama 3 also titled their 1997 debut release 'Exile on Coldharbour Lane' in tribute to their local street, and the album offers an unusual but fascinatingly rich combination of country music, blues and electro-pop that's a surprisingly good listen if you want to hear something a little bit different.

Although the little bit of Coldharbour Lane I've seen so far doesn't look too bad despite its reputation, I can see why the problems that led to its notoriety could have arisen. It is fairly unappealing aesthetically, with tightly packed flats and shops hemmed in by overhead railway viaducts that would have made it a very claustrophobic place to live. But as with most of what I've seen so far in Brixton, it does have quite a buzz about it and feels pretty quirky, with a mix of shops and cafes adding to the vibe of the street markets, all of which gives me the feeling that the area is considerably more positive than the Brixton of forty years ago.

Just after the entrance to Market Row I come across the site of another closed down record shop, the highly influential reggae and roots Blacker Dread's Muzic Store, which traded from 1993 until 2019 and was a

Rock & Stroll

popular meeting place and cornerstone of the local Afro-Caribbean community. Shortly after passing that I turn left into Atlantic Road and then left again, which takes me into the street that is the main reason for my visit to Brixton, as well as being the inspiration for one of London's most famous songs: 'Electric Avenue' by Eddy Grant.

So named as it was Britain's first shopping street to be illuminated by electricity when it opened in 1888, Electric Avenue was an early example of what we would now call a shopping mall. Classy and elegant, it consisted of tall Victorian shops that curved gently away from the main Brixton Road towards Atlantic Road, their frontages covered by cast iron canopies to protect shoppers from the elements.

Those canopies remained for nearly a century until they were removed in the 1980s and most of the upstairs rooms above them now appear to be residential flats, but as part of Brixton Market this is still an important local retail hub, specialising in ethnic Afro-Caribbean foods and various lifestyle products. This has made it one of the busiest market streets in London, so while it may not be as posh as it once was, that clearly hasn't made it any less popular as today it is heaving with people busily browsing the varied mix of shops and stalls. Enveloping this activity is a heady aroma of Caribbean cooking that lures me into buying a delicious Jamaican vegetable patty from one of the cafes. Not that I'm feeling particularly hungry, but I just couldn't resist.

While being famous to locals for years, it wasn't until Eddy Grant released the single 'Electric Avenue' in 1983 that the street found fame globally as it became a massive hit around the world. Written in response to the

Rock & Stroll

first Brixton riots, the song highlights the local tensions that existed at the time regarding racism, unemployment and poverty, and it played an important part in informing a wider audience of the need for change.

The song made headlines again in 2020, nearly forty years after its initial release, when Eddy Grant filed a lawsuit for infringement of copyright against Donald Trump's presidential campaign after they used it without permission for an election advert. I like Eddy Grant even more now. And after all this time, it's still such a well known song that it even influences the way people pronounce the name of the street, with the same intonation and rhythm as Eddy Grant that places the emphasis on the second syllable of e-LEC-tric. Try saying it in your head and I guarantee it will sound exactly like it does in the song.

Back in the early 1980s the heavy reggae electro sound of 'Electric Avenue' had a big influence on me personally as it contributed hugely to my love of reggae, an odd choice of listening at the time for a scrawny white teenager from the suburbs of Bedford. But then I never liked to follow the crowd, preferring instead to make my own discoveries, and so while most other kids at my school were getting into the likes of Adam and the Ants, Duran Duran, Soft Cell and Depeche Mode, I was listening to Bob Marley, Aswad, Black Uhuru and Eddy Grant. And oh my God, I've just remembered I even had that album by Musical Youth - pass the bucket!

Having been born in Guyana, Eddy Grant moved to London in the 1960s and before long formed a band called The Equals who had a hit in 1968 with the song 'Baby, Come Back'. Although a bigger hit for Brixton's

Rock & Stroll

own Pato Banton much later on, The Equals played the song on Top Of The Pops and as such were one of the first inter-racial groups ever to appear on the show.

While with The Equals, Eddy Grant also wrote the song 'Police on my Back' which was covered by The Clash on their epic 1980 triple album 'Sandinista!' (Yes, that's right, a triple album. You certainly got value for money in those days). And The Clash themselves have strong links with Brixton too, as lead guitarist Mick Jones and bassist Paul Simonon both grew up here, the latter having written and sung 'The Guns of Brixton'. This powerful reggae influenced punk song is often thought to have been written in response to the first Brixton riots, but as it was released in 1979 it actually predates them by a couple of years, a sign that local tensions were already rising and something big was likely to kick off. Despite its dark fatalism, 'The Guns of Brixton' is driven by an intensely raw but fierce sense of local pride in much the same vein as 'London Calling', the title track of the album on which it first appeared, with both songs being anthemic rallying calls for the oppressed and disillusioned in society to stand up and be counted.

Delighted to have visited Electric Avenue for the first time and happier still to see it thriving, I emerge back out onto the main road by Brixton tube station which marks the southern terminus of the Victoria Line. It also has the claim to fame that it exhibits the largest 'Underground' emblem roundel on the entire network which is set impressively in glass above its main entrance. But even that is dwarfed in significance by the idol just across the street, modestly tucked away round the corner into Tunstall Road beside Morley's department store. For

Rock & Stroll

here is a beautiful artwork dedicated to Brixton's own local hero, David Bowie.

Painted as a piece of graffiti art on the outside wall of the store, this popular mural depicts Bowie as another one of his alter egos, Aladdin Sane, in a similar pose to the one adopted on the album of that name and surrounded by a colourful array of floating planetary spheres. It was originally created in 2013 by Australian artist James Cochrane but became even more of a focal point for David Bowie's fans to gather after he passed away three years later. Thousands of flowers and souvenirs were left as it became a shrine to his memory, and many personal and passionate messages were written directly onto the mural itself. All this attention caused it to fade to a point where it had to be carefully repainted and it's now covered with a layer of Perspex to protect the work of art.

There are only a handful of mementoes honouring Bowie laid out on the pavement here today and, remarkably for such a busy location, it feels like an oasis of calm as it's just far enough off the main street to allow sufficient quiet and privacy for reverence and reflection.

Having admired this splendid image I progress northwards along Brixton Road and pass under another striking, yet far less conventional, piece of art - a railway viaduct gloriously painted in red, gold and green, bearing the messages "Come in Love" on one side and "Stay in Peace" upon the other. It's marvellous that something so drab and industrial can be turned into such a vibrant and attractive artwork.

A little further on I turn left into Stockwell Road and am immediately greeted by the wonderful Italianate domed entrance of the Brixton Academy. Over the years,

Rock & Stroll

this internationally famous concert hall has staged numerous major shows on its large fixed stage that is sumptuously framed by a design based upon Venice's Rialto Bridge. This makes it one of the most attractive and iconic live performance venues in the world, a fact recognised by the NME in naming it as Best Music Venue twelve times since 1994 and by the string of big stars who've performed here. Iron Maiden, Debbie Harry, Bob Dylan, Lady Gaga, Madonna and The Clash to name but a few, as well as The Smiths who played their last ever show at the Academy in December 1986. Many live recordings have also been made here, including album releases from Judas Priest, Gary Numan, David Gray, Dido, 5 Seconds of Summer and Franz Ferdinand, and promo videos too, which most famously include Wham's 'Wake Me Up Before You Go-Go' and Billy Ocean's 'When The Going Gets Tough, The Tough Get Going'.

Another notable live performance at the Academy came in June 1996 when electronic duo Leftfield rocked the house to its foundations with a sound system that was so loud it reached 137 decibels and caused showers of dust and plaster to fall from the ceiling. They were subsequently banned from playing the venue again, although the ban was lifted just four years later with the proviso that the incident wouldn't be repeated.

A little way past the Brixton Academy I see a small boy being pushed along in a Ferrari-red sports car buggy, living his best life making engine noises as his dad wheels him around. While stopped at a pedestrian crossing, dad takes the opportunity to educate him about the safe way to cross roads and the little boy listens intently before

Rock & Stroll

revving once more, desperate for the green man to appear so that dad can stick it in gear and get moving again.

"He looks like he's having fun," I say in passing.

"We both are," replies his dad, with an enthusiastic smile.

To my right at this point is Stockwell Skate Park which has a couple of teenage lads practising their skateboarding skills on the ramps, and pretty impressive they look too. Then to my left is Stansfield Road, a smart, tree-lined residential street that looks so ordinary it's hard to believe it played such a massive part in the history of rock music. For this unassuming street was the birthplace of one David Jones, aka David Bowie, who lived at number 40 until he was six-years-old when his family moved out to Bromley.

A short walk past Stansfield Road is Bowie's first school, Stockwell Primary, and as I pass by I try to imagine him as a small boy on the way to school, all smartly dressed up in his uniform. No doubt even at that very young age he was still more stylishly attired than his classmates, probably sporting a half-Windsor knotted tie, a well cut trouser and maybe a hint of eyeliner.

It could well have been around this time that he got the inspiration for one of his most famous creations, Major Tom, star of his 1969 mega hit 'Space Oddity', the song that set Bowie on the path to stardom. For it has been widely suggested that he came up with the character's name when, as a child, he saw an old poster featuring local Brixton music hall and circus performer Tom Major. Having remembered the name, he later flipped it around to create Major Tom. Whether that's true or not no-one seems to be sure, but it's a great story that's made even better

Rock & Stroll

when you also discover that Tom Major was in fact the father of former Prime Minister John Major.

Trekking further along Stockwell Road I can see the City of London skyscrapers in the distance, poking their wealthily coiffured and top-hatted heads above the flat-capped masses that lay before them. Among these are a significant number of Portuguese cafes and delis that reside along here, one of which has its door open and is playing some fairly traditional sounding guitar music as I pass by. I believe it's called fado, a type of folk music that originated in the Lisbon area, and it's telling me that I must be getting close to the neighbourhood known as Little Portugal. This is an area roughly between Stockwell and Vauxhall that is home to nearly thirty thousand Portuguese and Brazilian settlers and their descendants, one of whom is solemnly remembered at my next destination.

For here, at the main entrance to Stockwell tube station, is a memorial to Jean Charles de Menezes, the Brazilian electrician and local resident who was shot dead at the station by anti-terrorism police on 22nd July 2005 in a tragic case of mistaken identity. The shooting occurred the day after a series of failed bomb attacks in the capital which led to de Menezes being wrongly identified as a suspect and subsequently followed onto a train before being shot several times as it waited to depart.

This afternoon there are a few flowers at the base of the shrine which centres around a charming depiction of a smiling Jean Charles, surrounded by a colourful mosaic design that shines a ray of colour and hope over the whole dreadful affair.

From here, a mere stone's throw across Binfield Road, is another eye-catching monument to the sadly departed - the Stockwell War Memorial - which adorns the overground pillbox entrance of an old World War II deep level air raid shelter. One of several constructed beneath tube stations around London to protect residents from bombing, this particular shelter had become a dilapidated eyesore until Battersea artist Brian Barnes created this colourful mural that was unveiled in 1999 as a tribute to the fallen. As well as showing soldiers crawling through trenches and going over the top amid fields of poppies, it also features additional scenes of local significance based upon paintings done by pupils from Stockwell Park School. These include images of the Empire Windrush ship, Vincent van Gogh, who lived in the area for a few months in 1873, and of James Bond actor Sir Roger Moore who was born here in, as he often called it, Saint Ockwell.

      The memorial also commemorates the incredible Violette Szabo who grew up in Stockwell before going on to gain distinction during World War II as the first British woman to be awarded the George Cross for gallantry. Following the killing of her Hungarian-born husband by the Nazis, she sought revenge by joining the Special Operations Executive and training as an undercover agent. While on her second mission into occupied France, Violette was captured following a fierce gun battle where she held off the enemy despite being wounded herself, allowing one of her resistance comrades to escape. She was subsequently tortured by the Germans before being imprisoned at Ravensbrück concentration camp and later executed, bringing an end to this remarkable lady's life at just 23 years of age.

Rock & Stroll

Having been moved by the stories behind these memorials I disappear into Stockwell tube station to head back north of the Thames, but my brief sojourn across the water has taught me that there is most definitely nothing to fear from heading south. From what I've seen today it is incredibly varied and vibrant, particularly the Brixton area which appears to have pretty much reinvented itself from the image of a no-go area that was created around it in the 1970s and '80s into what is now a colourful fusion of art, music, markets and culture. It has both educated and thrilled me with its eclectic mix of sights and sounds; with its open, picturesque parkland; with its architecture, ranging from posh Italianate to Victorian and Edwardian Baroque; with artworks celebrating Jamaican heritage, a British pop style icon and tributes to fallen heroes; and through music, from reggae and glam rock to fado and punk.

Overall, I'm proud to say that I am leaving south of the river considerably better informed and with a far more positive image in my mind than the preconceived one I had when arriving. As some-time actor and governor of California Arnold Schwarzenegger once famously said: "I'll be back."

Rock & Stroll

Chapter 14
London's Brilliant Parade

There isn't very much that makes a man of my age and experience panic, but approaching a waiting tube train as it sounds the beep-beep warning that its doors are about to close gets me every time.

Luckily, I'm already stepping onto the platform at Stockwell station just as the bleeping starts so there isn't far to go, but even that short sprint gets my heart pumping and my mind racing through the options available to me were the doors to begin closing as I'm hurtling towards them. Should I continue to force my way in, risking getting stuck halfway and incurring the wrath of the other passengers as the train is delayed by the driver having to open the doors again to release me? Or would it be better to carry out an emergency stop, even though that could result in me headbutting the closing doors whilst simultaneously trying to look on casually as though I didn't want that train anyway?

On this occasion, I am fortunate enough to make it with a little time to spare and even have the luxury of being able to finish my sprint with a swagger, Usain Bolt style, to the only empty seat in the carriage. I sit down just as the train moves off, heading up the Northern Line, and

Rock & Stroll

only then do I realise why this seat is vacant: simply because no-one else fancied sitting next to the sloppy looking middle-aged guy guzzling a large phallus of a bratwurst from a paper bag. Funnily enough, I don't feel so smug about catching this train now.

Why do people insist on eating on the tube? It's so messy, incredibly anti-social and surely can't be all that enjoyable for the consumer either. Mind you, this bloke seems happy enough to be chomping away, oblivious to the fact that his lunch looks and smells utterly grotesque. Don't get me wrong, I like a bit of street food when it's appropriate, but in the unlikely event I should ever eat something that looks as awful as this sausage I would be sure to do so in the darkened privacy of my own kitchen, maybe with the fridge door slightly ajar to allow just the faintest illumination. I certainly wouldn't take it down onto one of the busiest transportation systems in the world and deep throat it.

In an attempt to ignore this gastronomic affront, I distract myself by looking up at the list of Northern Line stations displayed on the opposite side of the carriage and in doing so am reminded of several locations I had considered visiting for this project that didn't quite make the cut.

For instance, on the Charing Cross section of the Northern Line is Mornington Crescent which, being just one stop away from my starting point of Camden Town, only narrowly missed out despite punching well above its weight when it comes to cultural credentials. For a start, post-impressionist painters Walter Sickert and Spencer Gore both lived on this endearing little half-moon of a street. Perhaps even more famously it gives its name to a

Rock & Stroll

complex game on the long-running BBC Radio 4 panel show 'I'm Sorry I Haven't a Clue', in which the aim is to get to Mornington Crescent tube station via some imaginative tactics and an arbitrary set of rules. This strange game later became the subject of a jokey jazz composition by the wittily surrealist Bonzo Dog Doo-Dah Band.

In more music news, it also provided the inspiration and title of a song by Scottish indie band Belle and Sebastian which gives an account of the humdrum routine of city life, but told with an air of gentle optimism and an undertone of saucy suggestiveness. And London band My Life Story, who made their name during the 1990s with an interesting sound that fused Britpop with orchestral, also named their debut album 'Mornington Crescent'.

Moving up the Edgware branch of the Northern Line takes us to Hampstead, the setting for a record by West Ham born singer-songwriter-guitarist Linda Lewis, an often over-looked artist whose talent has seen her provide vocals for David Bowie, Cat Stevens, Rod Stewart and Jamiroquai, and earned her an appearance at the very first Glastonbury Festival. Titled 'Hampstead Way' after the leafy, upmarket avenue that borders the heath, as well as the location of a commune where she spent time living with several other artists, this 1971 release is a heartening reminder of her wonderfully crisp and elegant vocal style. It's a beautiful song.

Also set about here was Donovan's 1967 release 'Hampstead Incident', another typically hippy-esque offering which mentions visiting the historic Everyman Cinema on Holly Bush Vale while Hampstead Heath is

Rock & Stroll

shrouded in mist and rain - there he goes with the weather forecast again, but no sun this time, sadly.

Looking next at the High Barnet branch of the Northern Line, the first stop after the lines separate north of Camden is Kentish Town, the neighbourhood that contains the compact and bijou eatery Mario's Cafe. Well known for shunning the image of the traditional greasy spoon to instead become a provider of quality food and a gallery for local artists to display their work, this charming cafe was immortalised in song by London band Saint Etienne who also recorded the number 'Archway People', referring to the area a couple of stops further along.

Just another few short hops up the track is Finchley Central, used for the title of a 1966 hit by the New Vaudeville Band and which also happened to be the local station of the late Harry Beck, designer of the London Underground map. Inspired by electrical wiring diagrams in a way that only a technical draughtsman such as Beck could have been, his concept is still the basis for today's version, as are numerous other maps of mass transit systems around the world.

With Harry Beck in mind, I decide to reach into my backpack and take out my London street atlas in order to have a good look at the current edition of his tube map, as presented on the reverse of this pocket-sized guide in teeny-tiny letters that I can barely decipher. While delving into my bag I fight the urge to check on the progress of the sausage scoffer next to me, but fail miserably and have a quick look anyway. Happily, he has at last finished the bratwurst and is now wiping his mouth clean with the paper wrapper - well, at least he's making some effort to observe dining etiquette.

Rock & Stroll

Having taken out the map my eyes are naturally first drawn to my current position on the Northern Line, the vertical black conduit that shoots straight down the centre of the network like a spinal column; from High Barnet at the top of the cervical spine, with stations arranged like vertebrae as they pass through the bulging lumbar regions, past the new extension to Battersea that sticks out like a prolapsed disc, and all the way down south to the remotely dislocated coccyx of Morden. (Okay, that's enough spinal references - Editor).

Several other locations from this line are name-checked on the 2011 track 'Northern Line' by electronic music trio LV featuring Joshua Idehen, who freestyles his way through the stations and some of their features. But he'd have to go quite some way to beat comedy songwriter and YouTuber Jay Foreman, who can very impressively recite every single station on the entire tube network in a song whose lyrics consist entirely of just that, and to a remarkably fluent and catchy tune too. I've even seen footage of him performing the 'Every Tube Station' song live and, incredibly, he can remember the names of all the stations without needing a prompt sheet. Harry Beck would have been very proud.

Looking away from the Northern Line and around the perimeter of the tube map reminds me just how vast the underground system actually is, stretching well outside London into adjoining counties, and yet how wonderfully well it knits all these areas together. It's easy to think of London as being one great megacity and in doing so to forget that historically it consisted of numerous different towns and villages which, over several centuries, have morphed and mutated into one big, stodgy mass. It wasn't really planned out that way, it just happened. This gradual transformation explains why the individual look, the spirit and the culture of modern London can change so drastically from one district to another, a feature that I have certainly noticed while travelling around on this adventure.

While considering the general layout of London, I fully open out my street guide to look at the illustration showing Greater London as a whole and this gives me an even clearer idea of the scale and scope of the city. Once again, this serves as a reminder of several other notable musical locations dotted around the capital that I had circled in marker pen but then excluded from my trek due to them being too far out from the centre.

For instance, down in the south-east corner is Peckham which was a base for several members of Pulp in the early 1990s, shortly before they began to gain recognition at the dawn of Britpop. During that time they wrote and recorded the song '59 Lyndhurst Grove' in reference to a party Jarvis Cocker had attended at that address. Apparently he was ejected later in the evening, which no doubt livened things up a bit as the song makes it sound like an awfully dull party.

Moving round the map anti-clockwise I've marked the point where the River Lea makes its way through Stratford, not far from where it flows into the Thames at Bow Creek. Although far less well known than the Thames, this river meanders through large areas of North and East London and in doing so passes close to Tottenham, Adele's home town. Her experiences of growing up around the river inspired her to write the gospel flavoured 'River Lea' - a ballad that's as dark and

Rock & Stroll

deep as the river itself - which was released on her blockbuster third studio album, '25'. Quite a story for a humble little waterway that starts off in Luton, to later end up helping a megastar win a Grammy award.

Adele's first studio album, '19', also featured a song influenced by her teenage years in London, the beautifully poignant 'Hometown Glory'. Apparently written in just ten minutes, this powerfully bittersweet tribute to her birth city - part song of praise and part teen rebellion - is an incredibly moving composition, especially when you consider she wrote it while she was only sixteen-years-old.

A little further up the River Lea I've marked Evering Road, the street in Clapton that provided my fellow Bedfordian Tom Grennan with a place to live once he'd left his home town, as well as giving him the title and cover photo for his second album, released in 2021. Evering Road also has an infamous connection to sixties gangland crime, being the street where Reggie Kray murdered Jack 'the hat' McVitie in a basement flat. I bet the letting agent never mentioned that before Tom Grennan moved in.

On the eastern side of the River Lea, across from where Adele grew up in Tottenham, is the area of Walthamstow which featured in a 2012 song by that excellent Irish band The Cranberries. 'Waiting in Walthamstow' is an earnest tale of longing, set to a tune that has an almost tango-like feel and sung in the characteristically emotive style of the late, great Dolores O'Riordan. This part of North East London was also the home of hugely successful boy band East 17, who named themselves after the district postcode. And not content

Rock & Stroll

with that, they even gave their 1993 debut album the title 'Walthamstow'.

Just above Tottenham on the map is Edmonton Green which gave its name to the title of a song by popular local boys Chas & Dave. Lamenting changes that have occurred in the area during their lifetimes, this composition featured on the 1975 album 'Rockney', named after the Cockney style of rock & roll they originated after growing tired of trying to sing with American accents. And this opportunity to talk some more about this skilled duo, whose catalogue of work unapologetically represents London, is just too good a chance to miss.

Chas & Dave had a string of hits in the late 1970s and into the 80s yet were never really given the credit their talent deserved. Music purists were keen to dismiss them as a novelty act or as East End pub entertainers sporting flat caps and braces, but I always felt that was missing the point. Yes there were songs about rabbits, sideboards and Cockney profanities, but they were simply singing about what they knew from working class London, heavily influenced by music hall and skiffle. There was an infectious joy about their material as they proudly stuck to their roots in a style that had never really seen chart success before, or since.

They were also extremely underrated musicians. Chas Hodges had started out with a band called The Outlaws, which included Deep Purple guitarist Ritchie Blackmore, and before teaming up with Dave Peacock they were both renowned session players and support acts for artists such as Jerry Lee Lewis, Gene Vincent, Albert Lee and even The Beatles. In addition to this impressive list they recorded with the great Labi Siffre on his 1975

Rock & Stroll

song 'I Got The...', a track that featured Chas on guitar with Dave on bass, and which went on to be sampled some 24 years later by the legendary American rapper Eminem for his huge hit 'My Name Is'. So, in a round-the-houses kind of way, they can also claim to have worked with Eminem. Which means, astonishingly, that the next time you're chilling in the hood, flexing some badass rap down the crib with your homies, you might just be vibing a rad piece of Chas & Dave. True dat.

And if that's not enough to convince you of their pedigree, then maybe you'll be impressed by the fact that American superstar Tori Amos once recorded one of their compositions. This unexpected boost to their credibility as songwriters occurred during the 1990s when, while Tori was living in Swiss Cottage, she decided to get into the heart and soul of the city by covering their song 'London Girls'. Although this fact sounds so surprising it almost seems like an April Fool's joke, she actually delivers a very melodic, slowed down version that's a huge contrast to the boisterous rockney beat of the original and works remarkably well with her soulful vocals and sensitive piano playing. Pure class, and without a flat cap in sight.

Navigating down the map more centrally but remaining in the east, Mile End is surrounded by another big black Sharpie circle that marks it as the title of a song by Pulp that was included on the Deluxe Version of their album 'Different Class', as well as featuring in the soundtrack to the film 'Tainspotting'. Depicting the squalid living arrangements Jarvis Cocker and bassist Steve Mackey experienced in Mile End at the time, this is one more terrific example of Pulp's clever lyrics having the ability to show that the reality of life in London is seldom as glamorous and stylish as people often like to think.

Moving still closer towards the city centre and near Liverpool Street station is Norton Folgate, a short section of street that runs between Shoreditch High Street and Bishopsgate. Once part of a larger area just outside the walls to the ancient City of London, Norton Folgate was formed during the reformation when the local Priory of St Mary Spital was dissolved. This resulted in the surrounding land being granted the status of a medieval "liberty", meaning that it was able to operate independently from the neighbouring area and as such was free from the rules and conventions of the rest of the city.

Consisting of numerous alleyways and passages, The Liberty of Norton Folgate was managed by trustees and local worthies under the governance of St Paul's Cathedral, making it a largely self-dependent enclave throughout the 18th and 19th centuries with its own church, school, hospitals and a thriving silk weaving industry. This independence lasted until it was merged with the Borough of Stepney in 1900, meaning that its history as an autonomous region would have been all but forgotten if it wasn't for two things. Firstly, a row about plans for massive local re-development just over 100 years later uncovered documents indicating that Norton Folgate may still retain some of its rights to act as an independent entity; and secondly, the year 2009 saw Madness release an album that would introduce its story to the wider world.

'The Liberty of Norton Folgate' was Madness' first album of new material in a decade and was a huge critical success. It contains several songs pertaining to London and its people and as such has been deemed a concept album, being imaginatively supported with an in-concert film directed by Julien Temple. Both the album and the film are full of graphic vignettes of London life, with numbers such as 'We Are London', 'Clerkenwell Polka' and 'NW5', but it's the title track that really stands out as a tribute to the city. At just over ten minutes long, this epic musical account of the area's changing social history, from Victorian music hall, melodrama and migration to the modern day equivalent, shows that things perhaps haven't changed so much since the old days after all. It is without doubt one of the most intriguing songs ever written about London and could only have come from a band who totally understand the city; and it could only have come from a band that are as quirky and original as Madness.

Having been lost for some time in my musings I have only just noticed that my bratwurst buddy has since left the carriage and, even though some passengers are standing, there is now a vacant seat on my other side too. Obviously then, I must now be the annoying person on the train that no-one wants to sit next to, but at least that gives me more elbow room. So, with my street guide now stretched out across my knees, I can clearly see the district of Fortis Green circled in permanent marker up near the top of the map.

This little known piece of North London, nestled between Muswell Hill and East Finchley, is the area that saw the formation in 1967 of folk rock band Fairport Convention, who share the first part of their name with the family home of original member Simon Nicol. But it can claim a much bigger part in the history of rock music than that, for this neighbourhood was also the birthplace of Ray and Dave Davies, founder members and chief songwriters of The Kinks.

The Davies brothers were both born and raised in Denmark Terrace, Fortis Green, and even gave their very first live public performance at their dad's local pub, The Clissold Arms, which is directly across the road from their family home. Although that gig took place way back in 1960, the pub is still in existence today and proudly celebrates the historic event with a display of photographs and memorabilia to mark the band's association with the locality.

In honour of his place of birth, Dave Davies wrote a number called 'Fortis Green' that was included on his 1999 solo album of the same name which, in typical Davies style, is a character driven novelette of a song, full of anecdotal charm and nostalgia yet tinged with a little sadness and regret.

I think it's fair to say that nobody else truly embodies London like The Kinks. They're the band that all others from the capital look up to. Their style is profoundly British and unashamedly London, yet still relevant enough to charm the rest of the world through a catalogue of song titles and lyrics that convey the love they have for the city through countless references to various locales and facets of London life. As such, you've probably noticed they have featured in more chapters of this book than anyone else.

The Kinks are undoubtedly a national treasure.

* * *

Rock & Stroll

Moving further round the map to North West London, we find the world famous Wembley complex which has staged countless major music concerts at its Arena and Stadium, including the most important show of the lot - the global jukebox that was Live Aid. It was staged on the 13th July 1985 and although I didn't attend the concert in person, I watched every second of it on television and was there in spirit, along with pretty much everyone else on the planet.

This was such a special day, where we genuinely believed we could eradicate famine and change the world through the power music. It seemed easy enough, as Bob Geldof himself had told us in the wake of the Band Aid single that the cost of change was just "a piece of plastic seven inches across with a hole in the middle." Perhaps we were naive to think such a thing could be so simple but I'm sure some good came out of it, even if the positive effects didn't last as long as we all hoped they would. And for the twenty minutes that Freddie Mercury and Queen performed their set, the world of music actually did change as they produced what is generally accepted as being the greatest live performance of all time, setting the standard for stadium rock that all other bands are still striving to equal.

Down the way from Wembley Stadium (which, incidentally, has more toilets than any other building on the planet - an astonishing 2618), I have marked the site of Hammersmith Palais on Shepherd's Bush Road, the former entertainment venue that was referenced in a song by The Clash, another band who, like The Kinks, have an attitude and perspective that typifies London.

Rock & Stroll

Having appeared on the music scene a dozen or so years after The Kinks however, their body of work tends to reference life in the city from a very different angle. Whereas many of The Kinks' songs commented on the quaint and quirky aspects of London life, The Clash targetted much tougher and more rebellious subjects. Songs such as 'Capital Radio One', 'London's Burning', 'Last Gang in Town', the previously mentioned 'Guns of Brixton' and their seminal album 'London Calling' are all examples of the influence the city had on their work. This was especially heightened in response to the changing face of the country amid the social and political attitudes and aspirations kindled by Thatcher's Britain, all of which shaped much of their creative output, as was the case with many bands in that post-punk era. You can say whatever you like about Margaret Thatcher, but if it hadn't been for her we'd have missed out on some bloody good music.

That tough edge of The Clash is very well represented by the song '(White Man) In Hammersmith Palais', a rock reggae record that tells the story of Joe Strummer attending an all night reggae gig at this famous venue and being one of the very few white people in the audience. In typical Clash style, it's a raw, hard-hitting composition that bravely fuses musical genres while addressing issues such as right-wing extremism, racial unity, distribution of wealth, and even finding time to have a dig at some of the other, less competent, punk acts that existed at the time.

Sadly, all good things come to an end, as did The Clash in 1986, and Hammersmith Palais too, when its curtain dropped for the last time in 2007 after nearly one hundred years at the forefront of entertainment. It was subsequently demolished and replaced by a student accommodation block in 2013, imposing a sad finale onto one of the UK's most iconic concert venues.

Its demise was the subject of a song by former Hanoi Rocks front man Michael Monroe, backed by his aptly named band Demolition 23, which is in stark contrast to the Palais having been mentioned in happier times as one of Ian Dury's 'Reasons to be Cheerful' several years earlier. Furthermore, it is affectionately referred to in 'London's Brilliant Parade', Elvis Costello's richly textured portrait of the city that was a highlight of his 1994 album 'Brutal Youth' and which is, in my opinion, one of the most beautiful songs ever written about London.

Lyrically superb and vocally sublime, this exceptional song has a dreamlike quality that somehow manages to lift you to a point where you feel as if you're floating above the city, touring sites such as Hungerford Bridge, Kensington, Regent's Park, Camden Town and Olympia, all of which are mentioned in the song, along with a red Routemaster bus thrown in for good measure. Powerful yet understated and sentimental, this is one of Elvis Costello's finest recordings and a splendid tribute to his birth city.

There are, of course, numerous other worthy songs that provide snapshots of the city through its lifestyle and culture, many of which deal with London in more general terms rather than focus on specific locations. It's impossible to list them all, but here's just a few: 'Wild West End' and 'Portobello Belle' (Dire Straits), 'London' (The Smiths), 'The City' (Ed Sheeran), 'London Belongs To Me' (Saint Etienne), 'West End Girls' (Pet Shop Boys), 'London Town' (Laura Marling), 'North Circular' (Real

Rock & Stroll

Lies), 'Londinium' (Catatonia), 'Powis Square' (Ry Cooder), 'Cockney Translation' (Smiley Culture), 'Bus Driver's Prayer' (Ian Dury)....and many, many more. I'm very sorry if I haven't managed to include at least one of your favourites.

One more song that certainly does need to be talked about though, is 'LDN', Lily Allen's text-speak titled hit from 2006 that sees her travelling around the city to a cheerfully up-tempo Caribbean beat. It's a tremendously catchy number that cleverly juxtaposes its jaunty mood against the harsh reality of what often goes on behind the facade of everyday life when you look a little closer. Musically it's a great song, but the intriguing lyrics really steal the show as she views the events that are unfolding around her. This once more confirms the appeal of people watching in the big city, all observed by Lily Allen with the keen eye for detail of Ralph McTell's 'Streets of London' and told like a true wordsmith in the manner of Ray Davies and Ian Dury.

And among the priceless sights mentioned in the lyrics of 'LDN' she even finds time to speak of watching people eating al fresco, which makes me wonder if she might ever have met my friend the sausage scoffer? That vision really would have been one to treasure.

Rock & Stroll

Chapter 15
Waterloo Sunset

The final stretch of my journey around the labyrinth of London's musical treasures begins as I emerge from Charing Cross railway station and walk towards one of the most famous and historic sites of Central London - and it doesn't get much more central than this.

For here, in front of the ornate Victorian facade of the station, in the middle of the always busy taxi rank, is a tall stone column topped with a cross that marks the very centre of the city; the point where all distances to and from London are measured. Well, near enough anyway.

The actual point that's accepted as being the official centre of London is, in fact, a mere stone's throw away on the northern tip of Whitehall at its junction with Trafalgar Square, where now stands a statue of Charles I on horseback. But back in 1291 a stone cross was erected on that particular spot by order of Edward I to memorialise the final place that the cortege carrying the body of his wife, Eleanor of Castile, rested on its way to Westminster Abbey. This was one of twelve crosses beautifully crafted from Caen stone that were built in her honour to mark the funeral route down from Lincolnshire.

The location of the original cross was designated as being the geographical centre of London, thus giving its name to the spot that is technically Charing Cross. That

Rock & Stroll

cross however, was demolished by order of Parliament in 1647 during the English Civil War. So the stone column that stands in front of the railway station today is actually an elaborate replica that was designed by E.M.Barry in 1863 and is correctly called The Eleanor Cross. But as it is so close to the location of the original it is frequently, and quite understandably, referred to as being *the* Charing Cross.

All of which makes a far more romantic story and a much nicer way of marking the hub of the metropolis too, even if that means it is ever so slightly off-centre. But that doesn't seem to matter as I look up at this fine column today with so much activity circling its base, bringing to mind the spindle of a record player standing tall and elegant while the groove of London busily revolves around it, sometimes smoothly, but sometimes with a skip and a crackle.

Having admired the elegant stone work I exit the station forecourt and turn right to head east along the Strand, happily soon coming across a branch of Leon, my favourite fast food chain. I always find their imaginative food a great deal tastier than their competitors, as well as being more varied and ethically sourced, and as I'm feeling like a break I pop in for a coffee and a chance to sit down. But unfortunately, there are no free seats as it's swamped with the early evening hordes of workers grabbing a bite to eat before catching the train home. So instead, I opt for a take-away coffee and also fancy a lemon drizzle, but as there's a queue for the toilet I just settle for the coffee.

Upon leaving Leon, I switch my steaming hot Americano between my hands to avoid getting my fingers burned while continuing to walk along the Strand. Up until

Rock & Stroll

the mid-19th century this was the closest main road to the north bank of the Thames, hence it's name which is derived from the Old English word "strond", meaning edge of a river. Back then, the land leading down to the river was made up of a densely packed warren of dark, narrow lanes that gave access to wharves and jetties where ships would have docked and been unloaded. But that all changed with the completion in 1870 of Victoria Embankment, the construction of which led to increased gentrification as the area was quickly developed to became the site of several high class hotels, theatres, influential banks and grand churches. Add to that Somerset House, King's College and the Royal Courts of Justice, and the Conservative Prime Minister Benjamin Disraeli proudly declared it to be "perhaps the finest street in Europe."

Nowadays, while the grandest of those buildings remain, numerous others have disappeared and, similar to countless other London streets, the Strand is now dominated by mainstream retailers, restaurants and coffee chains.

Despite its rich history, it's quite disappointing to discover that there don't appear to have been many songs written about the Strand. I suppose the most famous one would have to be that old Edwardian music hall standard 'Let's All Go Down the Strand! ('ave a Banana)' - but that's about it. Presumably no-one ever felt able to better those lyrics, although Blur, weirdly, did record a cover version. Other than that, Sting wrote a piece entitled 'Ghost in the Strand', an appropriately haunting jazz instrumental number that was released as the B-side of his 1987 single 'Englishman in New York'. And Roxy Music's second album, 'For Your Pleasure', released in 1973, featured the song 'Do the Strand' which encourages a hip new dance craze. Although undefined, the Rocky Horror-esque style of the music suggests the dance to be overtly hedonistic, but it has to be said that the tune hasn't aged well and the lyrics sound very dated too. On the plus side however, it is almost certainly the only song ever written that contains the word "rhododendron" in its lyrics.

But then, about halfway along the Strand is something that played an even more important part in the history of contemporary music than a shrubby lyric ever could. To find it, I hurry past the front entrance road to the famed Savoy Hotel (incidentally, the only road in the UK where you're legally required to drive on the right) and then, immediately after Simpson's restaurant, I turn right to head down a dark, narrow alleyway named Savoy Buildings. This is just one of several Savoy themed lanes, passageways and buildings that dominate the area, and from there, having passed a guy having a cheeky slash against the wall (when you gotta go, you gotta go), I emerge onto Savoy Hill and turn left. This brings me to its junction with Savoy Steps, a rear access road to the hotel, which happens to be the extremely unlikely setting for what is considered to be the forerunner of the modern music video.

For it was here, in 1965, that Bob Dylan was filmed flipping through flash cards along to the lyrics of the song 'Subterranean Homesick Blues', a sequence which made up the iconic opening scene of the documentary film 'Don't Look Back'. The flash cards, which included a few deliberate spelling mistakes, were written out by Dylan with assistance from fellow folkies

Rock & Stroll

Joan Baez and Donovan, while he was staying at the Savoy during a break from his UK tour.

I'd always assumed that this promo film had been shot up some gloomy, decrepit dead-end alleyway in downtown Manhattan, rather than some gloomy, decrepit dead-end alleyway behind the Savoy Hotel. I'm sure most other people thought the same too. It really is amazing the unlikely places that you can discover a piece of music history, and you don't even have to stray that far off the beaten track to find it.

Retracing my steps, and treading very carefully, up the appropriately subterranean passageway of Savoy Buildings, I return to carry on along the Strand, crossing the junction of Lancaster Place to the right with Wellington Street on the left. As I cross and look up Wellington Street I can clearly see the grand portico that fronts the Lyceum Theatre, home to the excellent Disney musical 'Lion King' since 1999, and also the place where Bob Marley and the Wailers recorded their 1975 album entitled 'Live!'. Although not very imaginatively named, this groundbreaking record propelled Marley's roots reggae music firmly into the mainstream of popular culture as it sold massively around the world. It also featured the emotive 'No Woman, No Cry' which became a global smash hit single before later receiving the well deserved accolade of being ranked No.37 in Rolling Stone magazine's 'Greatest Songs of All Time' list.

Moving along towards the end of the Strand I pass by the grandeur of Somerset House, St Mary-le-Strand Church and the Royal Courts of Justice, the latter looking so resolutely sombre and formidably judicial that I immediately feel the compulsion to plead guilty, your

Rock & Stroll

honour. From there, I pass by the Temple Bar Marker statue to enter the City of London, via Fleet Street.

Named after the River Fleet, an almost forgotten channel that runs underground from Hampstead to the Thames, there is evidence of a route here dating back to Roman times which evolved over the centuries to become a major road connecting East and West London through the City. It's also one of the most historically significant, being the main ceremonial route that links the Tower of London and St Paul's Cathedral to Westminster and Buckingham Palace. As such, it has some marvellously impressive architecture that certainly befits its standing, with the large stone churches of St Dunstan's and St Bride's being particularly magnificent, as well as several banks and legal establishments interspersed with timber fronted taverns, wine bars, statues and intriguing alleyways. But the most striking thing I can see as I stride eastwards is the dome of St Paul's Cathedral, dominating the skyline ahead of me as it soars majestically over the City while all its neighbours peer out from the shadows in reverence at its splendour. It is a truly incredible view that inspires me to regain the spring in my step that's been missing as my legs have become increasingly tired during this long day of walking.

Aside from its fine architecture, Fleet Street will forever be associated with the printing and newspaper industries that brought global recognition to the area as they flourished from the 16th century all the way through to the latter part of the 20th century, when most of them moved out to larger, more modern premises. Compared to their huge occupancy of the street back in its heyday, there is little trace of them now, although some publishers retain

Rock & Stroll

a presence and a few buildings still bear plaques and other adornments that commemorate influential figures and events, as well as the names of the newspaper titles they housed. All of which, no doubt, guarantees that the street will always be inextricably linked to the industry.

A far lesser claim to fame for Fleet Street is that it also lent its name to the title of a song by a heavy metal band called Fist, which featured on their 1981 album 'Thunder in Rock'. It's a bit of a strange offering, not least because Fist come from Toronto, so not exactly local to the area, and the track starts very oddly. There are distant screams, the eerie sound of church bells and footsteps walking along a street before two voices start up an earnest conversation. They quickly identify themselves as being Sherlock Holmes and Dr Watson, admitting they're lost in the fog and trying to find clues as to where they might be. During this murky melodrama of an opening, Holmes naturally deduces that they must have inadvertently wandered into Fleet Street before the music starts up and drowns him out with the typically big, brazen power chords of hard rock. This makes it very difficult to understand the lyrics when they begin, even though the vocalist does his best to scream his lungs out over the top of it, all of which results in an interesting track that's definitely worth listening to if you love heavy metal. And if you don't, then it's not.

As the time is now moving into the mid-evening I'm feeling quite hungry and in need of sustenance, so I pop into a cafe next to a shabby looking barber's shop and order a meat pie to go. I'm served quickly as there's no-one else in there, and as I tuck into my pie while continuing

Rock & Stroll

along Fleet Street I can understand why they're so quiet. It's got to be the worst pie in London.

Just opposite the Nat West Bank I ditch the pie in a bin and turn right into Bouverie Street, a narrow lane hemmed in by modern office buildings that again used to house several major newspaper titles. I follow it to the end, past a long line of Boris Bikes waiting for hire, and into the somewhat grander and more refined looking Temple Avenue. Here, a film crew are packing away their gear into six large trucks at the end of a day's filming what I'm guessing, judging by the numerous extras milling around in Victorian period costume, must have been some sort of historical drama.

Temple Avenue then brings me out onto the wide open spaces of Victoria Embankment where I immediately cross the road, knowing that from the other side I'll be able to enjoy a terrific view of the multitude of modern skyscrapers over the river on the South Bank of the Thames. Despite all the brilliance of this architecture however, my favourite structure has always been the one that's directly opposite where I'm currently standing: the rather plain brick column with the cheeky windows that goes by the name of the Oxo Tower.

Nowadays part of a development containing upmarket apartments, bars, retail design studios, art galleries and a classy riverside restaurant, the tower is strikingly understated compared to most of the neighbouring buildings. This is hardly surprising when you consider it was originally built as part of a power station, before being purchased in the 1920s for use as a cold storage depot by the German company that produced Oxo meat extract.

Rock & Stroll

Keen to promote their product in this prominent location but prevented from doing so by strict rules on advertising beside the Thames, they came up with a cunning plan to overcome this obstacle. In what was literally a lightbulb moment, they realised that they could incorporate the brand name into the design of the structure with three huge, vertically aligned mosaic windows on each side of the tower in the shapes of a circle, a cross and another circle, thus boldly spelling out the name "OXO". And in case that didn't catch your eye, they had bright red lights beaming out from behind them as well, illuminating the river and its surrounds with the brand's corporate colour.

The company eventually vacated the building and it remained derelict until the mid-1970s when it began to be developed into the vibrant hub that it is today, but with the "OXO" logo still in place and proudly shining bright, though nowadays with more environmentally conscious LED lighting. I don't know about you, but I certainly can't think of a brand name of any other product that could so readily be turned into windows, and it's that history, along with its humble origins, that makes it such an iconic structure to this day.

Having stood and admired the scenery along the riverbank for a lengthy amount of time, I turn right and begin to amble along Victoria Embankment, probably my favourite London roadway. Wide and open, it provides splendid views across the Thames with endless sightseeing opportunities and historic landmarks along the nearly two-mile length that connects the bridges of Blackfriars and Westminster.

Rock & Stroll

Constructed in the 1860s under the direction of esteemed civil engineer Sir Joseph Bazalgette (whose great-great-grandson, Ed, happens to be lead singer on The Vapors' hit 'Turning Japanese'), this was part of an extensive project that involved land reclamation from the foreshore of the river, as well as the purchase and demolition of many nearby properties. The aim of this development was fourfold. Firstly, to cover the tunnels of the newly built District underground railway line; secondly, to provide alternative routes to ease the growing strain on the ever-busy Fleet Street and the Strand; thirdly, to straighten and partially narrow the river to help speed the flow of water, thus washing pollution away more quickly; then fourthly, and most importantly, having eased congestion in these increasingly clogged areas it allowed for the vital installation of Bazalgette's renowned sewer system to remove all the effluent and excrement that had been backing up. So Victoria Embankment can justifiably claim to be a relief road in more ways than one, and after 160 years this incredible feat of engineering is, thankfully, still very much up to the jobby.

Fortunately, the Thames in London is now in a far healthier state than when the Embankment was built. Back then, as well as being a sewage dump its usage was almost wholly based around industry and shipping, altogether making it so rife with disease and pollution that it was impossible for many forms of nature to exist. The rise in London's population and the effect of two World Wars perpetuated the problem to the extent that in 1957 the Natural History Museum declared the river to be biologically dead.

Rock & Stroll

However, significant changes to industrial and marine practices, allied with decisive action from wildlife authorities and governments, saw huge improvements in water quality towards the end of the 20th century. So much so that today it is one of the world's cleanest rivers to be flowing through a major city and wildlife that was once absent is now able to flourish. But it is still far from perfect, with the major threat to the bio-health of the river nowadays coming from increased quantities of domestic and commercial waste and discarded plastics.

Walking on along the Embankment, even though Joseph Bazalgette provided more than generous width across these pavements, my progress is still temporarily halted by a large group of teenaged American tourists taking multiple selfies. Despite this minor delay I am happy to see them enjoying themselves, even though I can't help thinking it might be nice if they would take an occasional photo of their surroundings too. After all, it's a long way to travel all the way from the States to then entirely ignore all these historic and iconic sites. They may never get the chance to see them again, whereas I think it's unlikely they'll ever forget what their own faces look like.

And these views really should be appreciated. I love strolling by the Thames. In fact, I love being beside any body of water, be it a river, lake, canal or sea. The sight and sound of water flowing is always so calming and peaceful, as is watching the plants and wildlife that rely on it in order to exist. No matter how turbulent or chaotic a place you may be in at the time, whether geographically or emotionally, it is endlessly therapeutic. I find it amazing how something that's vast and powerful enough to make

Rock & Stroll

you feel insignificant as an individual can also be so personally inspiring and life-affirming.

The Thames flowing through London also provides a welcome constant in the ever-changing, uncertain cycle of the city. This was referred to by Elton John in 2006 on a track taken from his 28th (omg!!) studio album, the critically acclaimed 'The Captain & The Kid'. This recording, which is an extremely belated sequel to the autobiographical 1975 release 'Captain Fantastic and the Brown Dirt Cowboy', contains several very personal tracks. Among them is the song 'Across the River Thames', written by Elton John and Bernie Taupin, in which they recount some of the career excesses they enjoyed as well as the lies they endured, and uses fog rolling across the Thames as a metaphor for order and balance. Other abiding symbols of London are similarly used in the lyrics to convey stability, such as Nelson's Column, London Bridge and Big Ben, which still proudly chimes out its existence, as do Elton and Bernie.

Further along the river and walking more slowly now - partly because I'm tired but mainly to enjoy the views - a song written by another Reg pops into my head. For as well as Reg Dwight (aka Elton John), contemporary folk singer Reg Meuross found great inspiration in London's landmarks for the endearing 'My Name is London Town' which features on his album 'Leaves and Feathers'. This entirely acoustic composition chronicles London with its many flaws and defects, as people's lives and events play out against a backdrop of the city's prominent locations. As he sings with melancholy acceptance of London with all its faults, he notes that it

Rock & Stroll

can be either your vision or your nightmare, depending on your station in life.

I have to confess that until I started researching this book I had never before heard of Reg Meuross or any of his material. I am happy to say however, that discovering 'My Name is London Town' has been one of the unexpected highlights of this project. This bittersweet and empathetic lament sums up the city so well, in much the same way that Ralph McTell did all those years ago with 'Streets of London'.

With late evening now approaching, streaks of sunlight are twinkling across the gently undulating flow of the river and glowing on the light grey Portland stone of the wonderful Waterloo Bridge which, although in the distance, is drawing ever closer.

This is a delightful view that has understandably inspired many artists to commit it to canvas, the most notable examples being John Constable's 'The Opening of Waterloo Bridge' from 1817 and several works by Claude Monet who painted many scenes of this area during frequent visits to London around the turn of the 20th century. In fact, so prolific was Monet's work throughout that period that he depicted Waterloo Bridge in over forty oil paintings, many of which were produced from his balcony at the Savoy Hotel and captured the subject and its surroundings in numerous different light and weather conditions.

All those paintings however, were of the old Waterloo Bridge which was completed just two years after the Battle of Waterloo, hence its name. During the 1930s that original was demolished due to having developed serious structural problems, leading to a new one having to

Rock & Stroll

be built. The construction of this replacement was delayed due to the onset of World War II causing difficulties with supply and labour, as many men were called up to join the forces. This problem was solved by training large numbers of women to complete the structure which finally opened in 1942, and to this day it is still affectionately known as The Ladies' Bridge.

This historic river crossing also gives its name to the area on the south side of the Thames that it leads into, as well as to Waterloo Station, the busiest railway station in the country. Furthermore, it marks the final point of my journey and, far more importantly than that, happens to be the location that inspired the most iconic song ever written about London: 'Waterloo Sunset'.

Released on the 1967 album 'Something Else by The Kinks', this song captures the quintessence of sixties London and remains one of that era's best-loved songs to this day. It's become an anthem for the city and in doing so has firmly established The Kinks as the poets laureate of London. They are constantly cited as being London's most influential band, having inspired the likes of Squeeze, Blur, Madness, The Jam, The Clash, Pulp, The Pretenders and many more with their narrative songwriting style and lyrics that abound with their obvious passion for the city. In addition, 'Waterloo Sunset' alone has been covered by a wide range of artists that includes David Bowie, Cathy Dennis, David Essex, The Jam, Peter Gabriel and Def Leppard.

'Waterloo Sunset' was written by Ray Davies, lead singer and principal songwriter of The Kinks, who was himself inspired by the setting as a young boy. Following medical treatment at the nearby St Thomas' Hospital

Rock & Stroll

which involved him having a tracheotomy, the nurses would often wheel him onto the balcony to look out over the river. From there he would watch the world go by, keenly observing London life from a distance.

This early experience of people watching no doubt nurtured his ability to compose lyrics that showed an empathy for everyday events, as well as the skill to record them with a journalistic eye for detail. This is evident throughout his work, but never more so than in 'Waterloo Sunset' which is poignantly narrated by the singer as he looks out from his window, watching in solitude as life passes by, illuminated by taxi lights and the dusky glow of sunset across the river.

Against this atmospheric backdrop, we are introduced to Terry and Julie who meet at Waterloo Station before crossing the river to get away from the crowds. Just like the narrator, they are happy to be in London but even happier to enjoy the simple pleasures of being alone. That's a feeling I'm sure we can all relate to, because as fantastic as London is, it's often a relief to escape the hordes of people and sensory overload that it subjects us to. Sometimes, it all just becomes too much.

In contrast to the understated reflection of the lyrics, the complex musical arrangement of the song creates a gripping mood that lures you in from the very beginning, so much so that on hearing its introduction you are instantly transported to this location. With its descending intro riff, instantly recognisable guitar hook and emotive vocals set against rising harmonies, it creates a sense of floating tranquillity that captures the ebb and flow not just of the river passing under the bridge but also the crowds of people crossing over it. All of which creates

Rock & Stroll

a spontaneous, colourful, textured piece of impressionistic art that's as much of a masterpiece as Monet himself created around Waterloo Bridge.

So strong is Ray Davies' connection to this location that he revisited it in the mid-1980s as the inspiration behind an album and short musical film entitled 'Return to Waterloo'. During the film, which deals with the isolation of a traveller who spends his daily commute daydreaming, Davies again observes what a lonely place London can be. This time though, he does so without the Terry and Julie that featured in the original song. I wonder whatever happened to them?

One thing we do know about them is that those characters were not named after Terence Stamp and Julie Christie, as is popularly thought to be the case. For although these two famous actors and gossip column celebrities were romantically linked at the time the original song was released, Ray Davies has always stated that this was purely coincidental.

Finally arriving at Waterloo Bridge itself, I cross the road by the RNLI lifeboat station (which happens to be the busiest one in the UK) and then climb the pedestrian steps that rise up from Victoria Embankment. These bring me out onto the bridge by Somerset House and I turn to head over the river, passing through the security barriers that stretch across the access pavements to most of London's bridges these days. Following the tragic terror attacks that have occurred in recent years, these are an unsightly but sadly necessary addition to this fine structure.

As I begin to walk across, a couple of young (and I'm guessing slightly pissed) ladies pass by me, loudly singing the ABBA song 'Waterloo' as they go. That gives me a great idea for my next music themed book: Eurovision winning songs inspired by 19th century battles. Okay, maybe it'll be more of a leaflet than a book.

Although The Kinks are rightly acclaimed for composing London's most revered song about Waterloo, there is another number dedicated to this landmark that is also well worth listening to. 'Waterloo Bridge', recorded by Louise Marshall with Jools Holland's Rhythm and Blues Orchestra, is a wonderfully arranged and lovingly sung composition with uplifting lyrics based on a poem by Wendy Cope. It's a beautifully bittersweet song that sees the singer crossing the river, light-headed on drink and charmed by music, before admitting to having fallen in love by the time she's only halfway across the bridge.

And what's not to love? The view from the midway point is so astounding it compels me to stop and admire the scene that stretches into the distance to the east, and then to turn around and look way out to the west as well. As the bridge was built at a bend in the river the views both up and downstream are unrestricted and breathtaking. From here you can see many of the sights I viewed from Primrose Hill at the start of my travels - though now very much closer - and lots more besides. St Paul's, The Gherkin, The Shard, Canary Wharf Tower, the London Eye, the National Theatre and Royal Festival Hall, Cleopatra's Needle, Big Ben, the Palace of Westminster, and an abundance of other notable structures all peeping out from the huddle and clamouring for attention.

In order to absorb the moment I rest my forearms on the parapet and gaze over the vivid landscape that's laid out before me like oils onto canvas - the remains of the late evening sun faintly shimmering on the architecture but still strong enough to cast long shadows across the rippled water; the glimmer radiating from windows as lights are being switched on, flecking buildings with a welcoming lustre; the heart-warming sight of buildings of all ages, styles, sizes and faiths mixing in harmony and comradeship. It's little wonder so many artists find inspiration in this city.

That inspiration is not to be found solely amongst these obvious landmarks and sightseeing spots though. Instead, it often appears in the backstreets and alleyways, which further confirms my long-held view that the fascination and enjoyment of London isn't restricted to just visiting its tourist sites and commercial attractions. It's also about seeking out its hideaways, discovering its secrets and observing its people.

Although the sun is now setting on my journey along the highways and byways of this city, my travels around all of the locations I've visited, be they popular or tucked away, have helped to restore my affection for the place. I have to confess that much of my faith in London has been severely tested over the last few years. Events such as the Grenfell Tower disaster, several acts of terrorism, increased violent crime involving weapons, a seemingly apparent rise in the incidence of civil unrest and demonstrations, growing numbers of homeless people on the streets and a general ugliness of behaviour and spirit have all challenged my perception of the city. Sometimes it's very hard to like London.

But during my research for this book and through the discoveries I've made on my musical quest around the capital, I'm pleased to say I have found that my fondness

Rock & Stroll

has returned and my faith is still largely intact. Yes, of course London does have its difficulties. It is an ever-changing city that has altered massively during my lifetime, possibly more than over any other similarly short period in its history. Change to that extent and at that speed inevitably brings problems. Therefore, it can no longer claim to be the swinging, carefree city of the sixties or the decadent glam rock capital of the seventies that many of the songs I've written about professed it to have been. In fact, I'm not convinced it ever truly was for most people. Like many things, that's probably just another one of those rose-tinted myths that gets handed down through the generations. Unfortunately, learning to accept that is not always easy.

However, through the power of music within the city I've come to realise that, as far as London is concerned, I have to take the rough with the smooth; the wheat with the chaff; The Kinks with the Des O'Connor. Because, as with music, not every aspect of London can be to everybody's taste - it is very much up to the individual. So while some parts are like a stadium filling rock anthem, others are a lonely, tear-jerking ballad. Some might be like a jaunty carnival reggae number or an improv jazz solo in a smoke-filled club, while others are a one-hit wonder, a little known album track, an unfinished symphony or an annoying novelty record that just keeps getting stuck in your head.

But wherever you are in London, you simply can't escape the music. It's everywhere you go, beating from its heart and pumping life through its arteries; in every street, road, tunnel, alleyway, avenue, park, passageway and

Rock & Stroll

garden. This enduring audio landscape is in the very DNA of the capital.

It's in the vibrant urgency of city life that sets a fast, metronomic tempo for you to walk in time with the backbeat that's present in the bass drone of all that traffic noise. It's in the percussion that's provided by the rhythmic clatter of building machinery and the steely clank of train on track. It's in the melody that comes from the buskers who brighten up even the dullest of tube stations, while the chorus is supplied by the constant background chatter of passers-by which is sometimes lyrically brilliant and other times loudly incoherent. And the album cover for this streetlife serenade is artfully depicted in the images all around you, with its people and its characters presenting a visual accompaniment to the soundtrack that's as vivid as any video on MTV.

And depending on your mood you'll hear pop or punk, funk or hip-hop, blues, reggae, heavy metal, ballad or soul, any of which can change from a bright and bouncy major key to a dark, discordant minor at the turning of a street corner. Because music expresses emotion in a way that words alone never can.

Modern London has that same effect. It can move you and it can challenge you in many ways, emotionally, intellectually and viscerally. It has become as diverse as it is perverse, somehow managing to be both repellent and delightful in equal measure. It's streets can be cruel - they can try your patience and they will certainly test your faith. But they will also entertain, educate and amuse you in a way that few other cities can. And that's the attraction that draws people in, day after day, year after year.

Rock & Stroll

Back in the year 1777, Dr Samuel Johnson stated that "When a man is tired of London, he is tired of life." Standing here on Waterloo Bridge at sunset, with The Kinks' classic song running through my head while relishing the glistening panorama of this city that means so much to so many people, at the end of an odyssey that has meant so much to me personally, it's impossible to imagine being tired of either of them. London does undeniably have many flaws, yet in spite of those shortcomings it manages to remain an amazing and captivating city that continues to influence and inspire...

...and London still rocks.

THE END

Rock & Stroll

Outro

London Pride

While much of the research for this book was carried out during 2019, including visits to the locations covered within the text, most of the actual writing was done throughout 2020 and '21 during the Covid-19 pandemic which saw the UK, along with the rest of the world, put into lockdown.

Obviously, this was an exceptionally tough and often heartbreaking time for so many people whose lives were affected by the virus, as it painfully reminded us that you never really know what you've got until it's gone.

Writing about London in these circumstances was extremely difficult as I had no way of knowing in what form the city I was committing to paper would exist in either the short term or the distant future. Regardless of this I soldiered on, knowing that London has coped with agony and despair in the past and certain that it would rejuvenate and re-energise itself as it has done before. In fact, I might even be bold enough to suggest that's what London does best, as it has an impressive track record of rebuilding itself and embracing the change and new opportunities that often result from hardship and adversity.

Rock & Stroll

Since writing this book I have revisited London several times and am pleased to say that much of what I knew and loved about the city before the pandemic appears to be returning, albeit a little slowly and cautiously. Inevitably, a few things have changed and that will no doubt be reflected to some extent in the music that is influenced by London. But whatever effect the uncertainties caused by the coronavirus pandemic may have, I am confident that things will be okay and the beat will go on. And not just for London, but for the UK as a whole, because it still has its heart, its soul, and its rock & roll.

Rock & Stroll

Acknowledgements

While the famous Chinese proverb "Every journey begins with a single step" is generally true, starting to write a book proved to be a far more complicated process. For me, that journey began with a mixture of fear, doubt and procrastination, a what3words combination that very nearly led to a location of failure. Diverting me away from that fateful place was not always easy, and so massive thanks are owed to certain people without whose help, support and patience this book would never have been completed.

      Firstly, my incredible daughter, Erin, for her help in editing the book, designing the cover and for patiently enduring me banging on about it all for months. Despite this, she always managed to remain interested and was especially supportive in the early days, even when I felt like quitting. Huge thanks also to Jacqui Hughes for her frequent music-based Facebook posts and her infectious love of Camden, all of which made me step up my game. To Sue Walsh for her encouraging words and for putting me in touch with Debbie Oliver whose enthusiasm for the project, allied to her skills as an editor and ability to point out things I had overlooked, have helped make this a more polished book and a far more fluent read than it otherwise would have been. And thanks to Simon Stabler at Best of British magazine for his kind comments and for allowing me to reproduce a modified version of an article I had written for them in 2019.

To my brother Paul for his amazing tech know-how and my other siblings, Judith and Noel, for their positivity and support; likewise to Alison, Hayley, Brett and Paige. Thanks also to Jim Russell for his love of music trivia and to the much missed John Coughlan, a skilled author himself who always encouraged my writing. Similarly, Geoff Roomes, that one teacher that makes all the difference, who taught me English as a twelve-year-old and gave me a love of writing that still thrills me whenever I have the chance to create something on a blank sheet of paper.

Finally, to my mum and dad, Audrey and Roy, who very sadly didn't quite make it to see this book in print, but were always supportive and, through their passion for crossword puzzles and Scrabble, passed onto me their love of words and language.

An idea is nothing if it cannot be shared,
so thank you for reading.

And to share further, please visit my author page on Amazon and leave a review to tell others what you thought of this book.

Rock & Stroll

Bibliography

Walk The Lines - Mark Mason, Arrow Books, 2011

The London Compendium - Ed Glinert, Penguin, 2004

Do Not Pass Go - Tim Moore, Vintage, 2003

In The City - Paul Du Noyer, Virgin Books, 2009

Between The Stops - Sandi Toksvig, Virago, 2019

The 100 Best London Songs - Time Out

Top 10 London Album Covers - Londonist

Part of Chapter 2 was adapted with permission from the article 'Warning - Beatles Crossing', written by Jon Askew and published in Best of British magazine, January 2019.

W·W
Worthy-Words

Rock & Stroll

Bonus Track

LONG WAY FROM THE JUNCTION- A SEQUEL

So many things have come and gone
Since that first windy night on Clapham Common;
A shy moonlit walk, her and me, hand in hand,
Loves young dream, in silhouette by the bandstand.

And I knew she'd finally fall for my charms
Back in the snug of the Railway Arms,
Where I cleared out the one-armed bandit,
Hitting the jackpot, just how I planned it.

We had such fun and so many laughs,
Our visions and dreams were a picture postcard
Of a life of love, lived in fields of clover,
Until the fun stopped and real life took over.

When she surrendered to that new army recruit
In his neatly pressed regimental dress suit.
I raised my voice and fists in protest,
But there never really would be any contest.

She left with our daughter to live by the sea,
Leaving Clapham behind, just to get away from me,
While I rebelled against the whole human race
And fell so fast that I sank without trace.

Rock & Stroll

Even though it's now the September of my life,
I still cry when I remember all of that strife.
Then I often wonder what on earth could have been
And think about the father that I should have been.

But despite all the anger, the hate and the tears,
The scars have managed to heal through the years,
So I've long come to terms with all of the sadness
And take pride today in my duty of dadness.

As I escort my daughter down the aisle
And glow in the warmth of her veiled smile.
In her bridal dress, she looks resplendent,
A beautiful young lady; strong and independent.

Guess it's all down to fate when life advances,
There's no time to hate when you've run out of chances:
So overwhelmed by the joy of this function,
We've come so far from those days up the junction.

Printed in Great Britain
by Amazon

From Camden Town to Waterloo Bridge, **Rock & Stroll** is a witty and informative walking tour that takes in the sights and sounds of rock and pop music through the streets of London. On the way it visits Abbey Road, Warwick Avenue, Baker Street, Soho, King's Road, Clapham Common, Electric Avenue and many other iconic music locations as it strides through the beating heart of the city.

Part passionate lament and part love song to the capital, this fascinating book explores London's enduring influence on popular music and blows the bloody doors off the many mysteries surrounding its connections to all musical genres, from rock, pop and punk through to reggae, jazz and folk: Where did Ziggy Stardust first fall to earth? Why was Bob Dylan feeling homesick in the Strand? Did Blockbusters host Bob Holness *really* play saxophone on Baker Street? Is The Beatles zebra crossing *still* The Beatles zebra crossing?

So if you've ever wondered where Jarvis Cocker fancies a late night coffee, why Eminem likes a bit of Chas & Dave, or exactly what is a bra vibrationer, **Rock & Stroll** will give you all the answers.

****

"If you like music, like London, or just enjoy watching its brilliant parade, then you'll love this book"

"One of the most captivating books about music in London"- Best of British Magazine

ISBN 9798408203734